DREADFUL DEEDS
AND
AWFUL MURDERS

By the same author:

Lady Policeman

Reluctant Nightingale

The British Policewoman: Her Story

Marlborough Street: The Story of a London Court

Tales from Bow Street

Blue Murder? Policemen Under Suspicion

DREADFUL DEEDS AND AND AWFUL MURDERS

SCOTLAND YARD'S FIRST DETECTIVES
1829–1878

Joan Lock

**BARN OWL
BOOKS**

© Joan Lock 1990

First published 1990 by
Barn Owl Books
Westowe Farmhouse
Lydeard St Lawrence
Taunton TA4 3SH
Somerset

British Library Cataloguing in Publication Data
Lock, Joan

Dreadful deeds and awful murders: Scotland Yard's
first detectives, 1829–1878.
1. London. Criminal investigation and history in
Metropolitan Police
I. Title
363.2'5'0941

ISBN 0–9509057–6–3

Designed by Tim Higgins
Typeset in Plantin
by Colset Private Limited, Singapore
Printed and bound by
Colorcraft Limited, Hong Kong

CONTENTS

'These games of chess, played with live pieces, are played before small audiences and are chronicled nowhere.'

Charles Dickens, 'A Detective Police Party', 1850

INTRODUCTION
The Birth of the New Police

FOR OVER 300 YEARS—up until the mid-eighteenth century—British policing relied mainly on unpaid parish or petty constables controlled by justices of the peace. The constables were locally selected for an annual term by their fellow citizens, but many bought their way out of their stint by hiring someone in their stead. Their numbers were augmented by often infirm or elderly nightwatchmen, or 'Charleys', but the ever-increasing and largely unchecked crime on London's streets demonstrated that the system was proving hopelessly inadequate for coping with highly populated urban areas.

Fortunately, successive Bow Street magistrates (Thomas De Veil and the Fielding brothers, Henry and John) took the matter in hand. De Veil—in office from 1739 to 1748—was courageous, determined, and tough in his fight against crime, had a flair for detective work, and was less corrupt than most other urban justices of the time. The novelist Henry Fielding and his blind brother John (who served from 1748 to 1780) brought honesty and integrity to the bench and, with the aid of Saunders Welch, high constable of Holborn, initiated what can be described as Britain's first detective force. They selected half a dozen permanent constables to be attached to Bow Street public office, who were to become known as 'Mr Fielding's people' or, later, as the Bow Street Runners. Operating in plain clothes, they were paid with complainant's fees and/or a share of the reward money after a conviction. Their freedom of movement and increasing knowledge of the underworld, together with their growing expertise, contributed to their success; and many, like Townsend, Ruthven, and Lavender, became widely known and respected.

By 1795, seven similar police offices had been authorized for central London locations: Great Marlborough Street (Soho), Queen Square (Westminster), Hatton Garden, Lambeth Street (Whitechapel), Worship Street (Finsbury), Union Hall (Southwark), and the Thameside, Shadwell. Wapping, just west of Shadwell, was added later, employing 80 river constables who were to become the Thames Police. Like Bow Street, each of these police offices had three paid justices, who combined the role of examining magistrate and police chief, and half a dozen paid police officers or Runners. Again, some of these caught the public eye; when mentioned by the Press, their names were usually linked with their place of service: 'Plank the officer of Marlborough Street', 'Lea of Lambeth', and so on. Bow Street also initiated the uniformed horse patrols and foot patrols which were eventually successful in ridding London's outskirts of highwaymen, and also helped in making the inner streets of the capital safer at night; and it was to remain the pre-eminent police office.

By 1828, London boasted several hundred assorted paid police officers (some of them part-time), in addition to parish constables and nightwatchmen, but they were still not enough. Serious pressure for a larger, more organized force had begun with the Ratcliff Highway murders in 1811, when a shopkeeper named Marr, his wife, their young baby, and a 14-year-old boy assistant were brutally murdered in their home. The area (slum-ridden Shadwell) had achieved notoriety with a recent run of six unsolved murders, and although patrols and Runners from other police offices joined in the hunt, most of the numerous suspects arrested and questioned were released by the time another local family was found slaughtered. Panic reigned — aggravated by the fact that no one seemed to be in overall charge of the investigation. Eventually a promising suspect was arrested, but he committed suicide before he could stand trial.

Lack of public order was another cause for concern. Political unrest (due to the depression which followed the long war with France) caused rioting in London on a scale with which the Runners and patrols were unable to cope, and troops had to be called in. An 1816 Select Committee on police revealed corruption in, and lack of co-operation among, the various factions. In the same year, an officer of the Bow Street foot patrols was found guilty and hanged for inciting robberies in order to catch the culprits.

The bungling of the arrest (by a Bow Street magistrate) of the Cato Street conspirators, who had been planning to assassinate the Cabinet, and further uncontrollable rioting during the early 1820s set the scene — firstly for an increase in patrols and general tightening up of the system, and, eventually, for the appointment of a Select Committee on police in the metropolis. Led by Sir Robert Peel, the Committee was convened in 1828, and the outcome was Peel's 1829 Police Bill, which was given royal assent on 19 July of that year. This allowed for the setting up of a centrally controlled metropolitan police force, with a strength of 3,000, to be led by

William Anthony, one of the last of
the London Watchmen or 'Charleys'.

two commissioners directly answerable to the Home Secretary. Once sanctioned, the New Police came into being with amazing rapidity. The first officers marched out from their six station houses (including one in Great Scotland Yard) on 29 September 1829.

The two commissioners (both Irish), who had the task of conjuring this new force from nowhere, were an ideal combination: the middle-aged, successful ex-soldier, Colonel Charles Rowan CB, an Ulsterman who had fought with Wellington at Waterloo and was accustomed to organizing men and maintaining discipline, and the energetic and innovative 32-year-old son of a Dublin judge, barrister Richard Mayne, who had been making a name for himself on the northern circuit. Their office at 4 Whitehall Place, Westminster, was actually in the front half of the same building as that of the new A (Central or Whitehall) Division station house, which opened onto Great Scotland Yard.

There were to be 17 divisions, extending over 7 square miles from Charing Cross. Each was to have a complement of 144 constables controlled by one superintendent, 4 inspectors, and 16 sergeants. The stated primary object of the New Police was the prevention of crime. The hours were to be long and the pay low. The recruits tended to be ex-soldiers, labourers, artisans, and some ex-foot patrols, and their uniform was deliberately low-key and unmilitary: swallow-tailed dark blue coat and trousers (with white trousers for summer wear), a stiff collar and leather neck-stock, and tall, reinforced top hat. In their pockets the constables carried a rattle, and hidden under their coat-tails, a short truncheon. (The Bow Street horse patrols, who continued to operate beyond the New Police borders, were armed with sabres, pistols, and truncheons, and carried handcuffs, and the Runners also armed themselves with cutlasses and a brace of pistols when they thought it necessary.)

One important asset the new force lacked was a detective branch. In fact it was to be another 13 years before one came into being, and this followed pressures similar to those under which the Runners and the New Police were born (although there is evidence that the commissioners, particularly Mayne, were merely biding their time). Meanwhile, the largely inexperienced uniformed officers had to cope with investigating crime as best they could—learning as they went along. Some attained sufficient skills and experience to be subsequently selected for the coveted posts in the detective branch.

Even when the New Police acquired their detective department, the numbers employed remained amazingly small for many years. In consequence, the experiences of these select few became wide and intense — small wonder they fascinated Charles Dickens and Wilkie Collins, authors who were to immortalize them. In this book, I follow the stumbling steps of the fledgling detectives, taken against a backdrop of severe Press criticism, intense public interest, and frequent antagonism from magistrates, coroners, lawyers and even prison governors. Compared with the CID of today, they were also much hampered by the lack of scientific aids (for example, the New Police were to be in existence for 70 years before the introduction of fingerprinting). There were no photographs to aid identification, communications were poor, and means of transport limited, although some of these factors were to alter dramatically during the service of the first detectives. Surprisingly, they did also have some advantages. For instance, widespread poverty often meant that a murderer was unable to change out of his bloodstained clothes, simply because they were the only garments he owned. But, then again, there was no positive test to identify bloodstains.

Conditions of the times affect not only methods of murder (throat-cutting with open razors and knifings were common in the early Victorian era) but also the murder scene — witness the 'candle factor' in chapter 4. Motives, too, differed from today's — more people were killed for money, less for sexual reasons. Several of our stories will be new to most readers, and even those which are better known will be seen through new eyes — those of the men who had the difficult job of seeking out the culprit, rather than the lawyers who had the facts handed to them in neatly tied briefs or the all-knowing Press. Where possible, the material has been culled from the hand-written reports and sometimes almost indecipherable notes in police files, from contemporary newspaper reports covering the lead-up at coroners and police courts (rather than relying merely on trial reports which rarely tell the whole story), and from other contemporary accounts.

The first detectives faced many challenges — and had their fair share of triumphs and tragedies. After 35 years their department was to be disgraced (by second-generation detectives) in the Turf Fraud scandal; but in this early period, these determined and often brave pioneers have some fascinating tales to tell.

PART I
THE LEAD-UP

1

IDENTITY CRISIS

THERE WAS SOMETHING not quite right about the body, thought the King's College porter, and he had seen quite a few in his time. Mr Partridge, his anatomist, liked subjects to be fresh, for obvious reasons, but this one seemed almost *too* fresh, and the way the left arm was bent and the fist clenched was unusual, to say the least.

But the new college had done business with at least one of the suppliers before. The 33-year-old John Bishop was a well-known 'resurrectionist', as was another of the four men, James May, alias Jack Stirabout or Blaze Eye Jack. The likes of Bishop and May did not always resort to digging up bodies. They would take lodgings near bereaved families, or those with terminally ill members, with the intention of doing business. Then, if a deal was struck, it saved the relatives the costs of burial. Should they refuse, the bodysnatchers were likely to sneak in and take it anyway, or follow the funeral cortège and seize their moment.

But this body did not look as though it had ever been laid out, nor was there any sawdust clinging to it — which was usually the case with those removed from coffins.

When Bishop and May had called earlier, on that Guy Fawkes Day in 1831, the asking prices had been twelve guineas. Bishop, on learning it was not a seller's market at the time, had agreed to ten; but Mr Partridge, through Hill the porter, had then refused to go higher than nine. May had not been pleased, and had said he was damned if he'd let it go for that price. 'Never mind May, he's drunk,' Bishop had murmured, adding the promise, 'It shall come in for nine in half an hour'.

It was three hours later when Bishop and May returned with another shady character, one Thomas Williams, and Michael Shields, a Covent Garden porter, who carried on his head a large basket out of which he tipped the rigid body of a 14-year-old boy.

The teeth had been removed. Nothing unusual in that. Dentists paid good money for them, for making up into false sets. But it seemed the boy had bled when it was done; his face was strangely swollen and his eyes bloodshot. Hill enquired what the boy had died of, and was told that it was neither his business nor theirs. He did not go so far as to enquire where they got the body from. That was not done. Too many questions and the supply might dry up, and there were few other ways for anatomy schools to acquire bodies. So they were forced to deal with unsavoury characters such as these in their smockfrocks and neckerchiefs, or greasy and worn workman's coatees, corduroy knee-britches and boots.

Of course, since the case of Burke and Hare only two years earlier, they had had to be a bit careful. When the notorious Scottish resurrectionists had been caught producing their own 'subjects' instead of bothering to dig them up, Dr Knox, the anatomist who had closed his eyes to the clues, had come in for a great deal of criticism, not to say abuse.

Hill was uneasy and asked the four men to wait. Mr Partridge was in no great need of a subject, so Hill could afford to be choosy; but in any case he was not happy about this particular body. After a quick examination Partridge shared his doubts but boxed clever, telling the men that he *would* have the body but that they would have to wait while he got change for a £50 note. Bishop said he would take what money he could see in Partridge's purse and come back on Monday for the rest, but the anatomist would have none of that. He had already alerted the College Secretary who, in turn, had sent an urgent message to one of London's then most famous policemen, Joseph Sadler Thomas, Superintendent of the F Division who had had marked success in handling unruly mobs during the first two tricky years of the New Police.

Bishop was also a little drunk, so his initial fears and suspicions were partially allayed, and he was soon buttonholing Hill with a proposition. If the porter handed over only eight guineas in the presence of the others, then slipped Bishop the other guinea in private, he would drop him half-a-crown for his trouble.

The F Division headquarters were in Covent Garden—only a short distance away—and the posse of policemen Thomas dispatched arrived before the four nervous men took flight. When they realized that their indecisiveness had led to a terrible error of judgement, they resisted arrest quite desperately. May was still struggling as he was carried into the police station—quickly followed by the hamper containing the body.

Superintendent Thomas had been fortunate in acquiring both a body and some prime suspects in one package, but what he did *not* have were any trained detectives to make the most of these unusual advantages. It had been difficult enough to get the freedom-loving British public to stomach a police force at all without asking them to accept 'plain-clothes police spies' such as those employed by the French.

In 1828, the year before the setting up of the New Police, a translation of the memoirs of Eugène François Vidocq had been published in London. The book described how this French ex-gaolbird had become head of the Sûreté by using his knowledge of the underworld to trap fellow-thieves. Worse, in September 1829, only two months before the New Police took to the streets, a melodrama, *VIDOCQ! The French Police Spy*, was staged at the Surrey Theatre.

It is true that the Runners were plain-clothes detectives (and were still operating as such in 1831), but their numbers and scope were limited, the public were accustomed to them, and they were great self-publicists. So, apart from a few plain-clothes officers on each division being sent out to catch pickpockets, the New Police had no detectives. When it came to a serious crime such as murder, the Divisional Superintendents and their uniformed inspectors had to cope as best they could while continuing with their other duties. Three of the early homicide victims proved to be their own men. Two of these cases required little detection, the policemen having been struck down by an incensed mob. But the third, the stabbing of PC Long by some suspicious persons he was questioning, was so badly handled that, according to one historian, the wrong man (who just happened to be nearby) was hanged.

Superintendent Thomas placed his prisoners at the bar in the front room of the old Covent Garden watch-house, which was now his F Division headquarters, and asked them what they had to say in answer to a charge of having improper possession of a dead body. The young and good-looking James May claimed the body 'belonged' to Bishop, while he had just helped him move it and kept him company. The middle-aged Michael Shields said he was only a hired porter, while ex-gaolbird Thomas Williams (whose real name was John Head) insisted that he had merely been curious to see what the new King's College was like.

Bishop actually admitted that the body was his. He had snatched it, he said, from Guy's Hospital mortuary — another trick his kind got up to. Thomas immediately sent around to Guy's, to find out who had died there recently, and was told that there had been only two male deaths in the previous week and these had been of men aged 33 and 37 — no boys. However, Bishop was telling a sort of truth in saying he had got the body from Guy's. He and May had left it there the previous evening after the hospital had declined to purchase. They and 'a porter' had collected it that morning, Thomas learned.

He then had the body brought in and placed on a table before the accused, pointing out the deep finger marks on the left wrist, the breast-bone which looked as though it had been forced in, and the cut over the eye. But Bishop stuck to his story, and claimed that the cut had been been caused when the body had been tipped out of the sack at the College. Partridge, the anatomist, had sounded the alarm but was unwilling to help Thomas further by agreeing that the boy must have been murdered. He conceded, however, that he certainly did not appear to have died a natural death. That was enough for Thomas. The next stop was before the magistrates at Bow Street.

Superintendent Thomas's relationship with Bow Street was curious, and one not entirely approved of by his commissioners, Rowan and Mayne. Throughout the two-year period before the setting up of the New Police, Thomas, a tradesman and a friend of the Radicals Francis Place and Leigh Hunt, had been parish constable for St Paul's, Covent Garden, and as such had brought his cases before the Bow Street magistrates. He had taken his duties more seriously than most of his kind — trying to clean up the area on behalf of his householders while at the same time attempting to obtain financial assistance for those in need — and attracting Press attention in the process. The Bow Street Runners had not appreciated his zeal and popularity, and even arrested him on one occasion on a trumped-up assault charge. But Mr Birnie, one of the Bow Street magistrates, mindful of the Press interest at this sensitive time of their waning powers, would have none of their squabbles and threw the case out.

The decision to appoint Thomas as Superintendent of the F or Bow Street Division while Bow Street still had its own Runners may have been sensible inasmuch he knew the area and was an honest man, but it was provocative none the less, and one which the commissioners had had some cause to regret. Eight months after his appointment Thomas received a tart letter from Mayne reminding him who was supposed to be in charge of the New Police. They had noticed in *The Times* that morning, Mayne said, that he had been asking the Bow Street magistrates what to do about dogs on the streets (too many roaming around, to the annoyance and danger of the public, he had claimed to magistrate Mr Minshull).

The Commissioners have more than once had occasion to notice the irregularity of such a course, and acquainted Mr Thomas that he was to apply to them in all cases, when he required any advice for the guidance of the Police. The Commissioners now desire Mr Thomas to understand that if they find him again repeating this practice, they will consider it a wilful disobedience of their orders.

On the evening of Saturday, 5 November 1831, Thomas placed Bishop, May, Shields, and Williams before Mr Minshull, an emotional but good-hearted Bow Street magistrate who was constantly surprised by the iniquities perpetrated by those brought before him.

'Did you not enquire of the men how they got possession of a body so fresh as they described?' he now asked Partridge.

'No,' replied the anatomist and added — bravely, considering the simmering hostility among the public in the packed office — 'We never ask that question. We are not in the habit of doing so.'

Superintendent Thomas got the remand he requested to make further enquiries, Minshull instructing that the four men be held at two different prisons and on no account allowed to communicate with each other. They left the bar to the hisses of the public, who had not failed to notice that it was always the poor who were at risk of being 'burked'.

The conduct of the police was beyond all praise, the *Observer* assured its readers the next day, and they were making every exertion to trace the last appearance of the deceased boy.

Identification of the body was Thomas's first big problem. Of course, there was no photography, photofit, or fingerprint technology to assist him, and there was a large homeless and anonymous street population to confuse — but one which did have its own internal society. He lost no time in circulating handbills with the description of the body of a healthy four-teen-year-old boy, about 4ft. 8in. tall, with a fair complexion and hair and grey eyes. Even Superintendent Thomas was surprised by the reaction. It was, he told the inquest jury the following week, perfectly astounding how many parents had lost a fourteen-year-old-boy — but none had been able to identify this body so far.

Early Press reports homed in on rumours that the description sounded like that of an Italian boy who was sometimes employed 'colouring images' and who otherwise wandered around 'showing' a tortoise and white mice. Once dubbed 'the Italian Boy', so the victim was to remain.

Thomas had received a letter saying that the Italian Boy's tortoise was on sale in Middle Row, Holborn. The shopkeeper, when traced, declared her husband had got it at Leadenhall Market where such things were regularly

Dean & Munday Litho' Threadneedle S'

The New Police searching for more bodies at
the home of the 'Italian Boy' murderers, 1831.
Probably from a broadsheet. (Courtesy of
Tower Hamlets Local History Library and Archives)

bought and sold. None the less, the Superintendent produced the creature at the inquest, where a witness declared it to be 'very similar' to the one carried by the Italian Boy.

Another witness, was stockbroker Mr Charles Starbruck, who assured the court that the body was indeed that of an Italian boy whom he and his brother often stopped and chatted to in his own language. They had seen him only last Thursday 'sitting on the pavement with his head nearly on his lap'. Mr Starbruck had thought the boy ill but his brother, who was the linguist, thought he was merely after the sympathy (and cash) of passers-by.

It was agreed that further enquiries were desirable, particularly about the purchasing of tortoises, and the inquest was adjourned for a couple of days.

The post mortem findings were not much help to the police. The surgeons were obviously puzzled as to the cause of death of such an apparently healthy boy. They did find evidence indicating a blow to the back of the neck and some of them were prepared to speculate on this, one telling the inquest jury that it was quite possible, indeed it was his opinion, that the boy had been first stunned by a blow on the back of the neck, and his neck afterwards twisted and dislocated like a duck's. At which, the *Morning Chronicle* told its readers, 'A thrill of horror here ran round amongst the crowded auditory'.

Thwarted here, Thomas began, rather belatedly, to concentrate on the four men in custody. He sent P C Joseph Higgins to the Fortune of War, a pub near St Bartholomew's Hospital known to be a haunt of body-snatchers. There he found the wives of Bishop and Williams and got them to take him to their primitive cottage, 3 Nova Scotia Gardens in Bethnal Green. (The relationships of these four were complex. On his father's death Bishop had married his stepmother, and then Williams married Bishop's sixteen-year-old stepsister. This meant that Bishop was both stepfather-in-law and stepbrother-in-law to Williams.)

Among their belongings P C Higgins found two wrenches and a chisel and told Mrs Bishop that he knew what *they* were for (opening coffins). He might well do so, she replied, but she didn't want him mentioning it in front of the children — a droll nicety under the circumstances. Higgins also found a bradawl with dried blood on it which had probably been used for punching out teeth.

But Bishop had already admitted that he was a bodysnatcher and that this body belonged to him; his tale now was that he had dug it up from a graveyard but could not say where, lest he get the watchmen into trouble.

More helpful was the Fortune of War barman, who said he had seen Bishop polishing some teeth with a silk handkerchief in the pub on the evening before he took the body to King's College. Police managed to trace the dentist who later bought them from May — for 12*s*. 6*d*. — and he had been told they had just been drawn *from a body which had never been buried*. The surgeons thought the boy's teeth had been drawn shortly after death. Now, things were starting to happen.

A week after first bringing in the accused, Thomas produced the teeth at Bow Street, where he got into a huddle in a private room with Mr Minshull and Mr Corder, the local vestry clerk. They emerged to make enigmatic announcements, Mr Minshull observing that he thought that they were now 'in the "thickest" part of the horrid affair' and Mr Thomas agreeing, adding that he hoped the guilty parties would soon be brought to justice. Which sounds rather like the statement of an onlooker rather than the man in charge. They did have some fresh evidence, Mr Minshull revealed, but publicity might jeopardize it, so all would be revealed a week later when the accused appeared again.

By now, Mr Starbruck had seen *his* Italian boy alive in the street, but Mr Corder told the court that he had ascertained that the victim was, none the less, an Italian boy. (There were a great many in London, owing to dire poverty in the corrupt Italian states.) This one's name was Giacomo Montero, and he had been left behind in this country by his master.

A week later, Thomas produced neighbours who swore to seeing 'an Italian boy' near Nova Scotia Gardens just before the murder was thought to have been committed. Others had seen men carrying out a sack on the following evening (Friday). A PC swore to hearing Bishop (after reading a handbill offering rewards for evidence against them) say, 'It is the blood that sold us' — but there was little other new evidence.

Mr Minshull declared another week's remand — to await the arrival of Augustine Brun, an Italian living in Birmingham, who had been the master of another Italian boy named Carlo Ferrari, who was now thought to be the victim. Mr Brun arrived later that evening, and an exhumation order was issued.

Mr Brun said he was fairly certain that the body was that of the boy he had brought over from Piedmont two years earlier and had then bound over to a man who travelled about the country, though he admitted he could not bear to look upon the boy's face as the thought of it grieved him so.

The New Police may have had little forensic aid, but Superintendent

Thomas was also very slow in initiating what he called 'a more rigid search' of Nova Scotia Gardens. He now put this right and found a brown, hairy cap which witnesses promptly identified as the one worn by the boy seen near the house. He also got PC Higgins to dig up the garden of No. 3, where they found more clothes, some of which were also recognized as belonging to the boy seen nearby. Inside the premises they found part of a suit, which according to the *Morning Chronicle* report had obviously belonged to a boy 'of very respectable family', and in a privy the hair and scalp of a woman.

Thomas hastened back to Bow Street, where he told the magistrates that he wanted to prefer further murder charges against the accused—of a person or persons unknown, further details to be forthcoming—and to dig up the gardens in the surrounding property. He was having great difficulty in stopping the vast crowds knocking down the cottages by their sheer weight of numbers, he admitted, and to ease the crush the owner, who lived in No. 1, had agreed to let people view the interior, four or five at a time, 'on payment of a trifling sum'. This announcement was obviously in response to a previous report in the *Morning Chronicle* hinting that it was the police of F Division who were doing the collecting.

In the event, Shields was released as not having been involved—though he had to fly for his life when spotted in Covent Garden—and Bishop, May, and Williams were at last committed on the charge of murdering Carlo Ferrari.

The trial took place in a packed Old Bailey court room before a bench crowded, as was usual in such cases, with people of note, including Prince Augustus Frederick, Duke of Sussex and sixth son of George III, and a man who took a great deal of interest in the law and social welfare. Taking shorthand notes of the whole proceedings (it is claimed[1]) was the 20-year-old Charles Dickens.

Police produced a stream of witnesses who brought together some of the other strands of circumstantial evidence. For example, there had been a slight smell of rum in the boy's stomach—and the men were proved to have purchased a quartern of rum just before the time of the suspected murder. A neighbour had heard scuffling on the night in question; Bishop's children had been seen playing with white mice soon after. Thomas had done a good job with his witnesses—though the possibility of a reward on conviction did tend to encourage total recall.

[1] Anon, *Burking the Italian Boy*—see Select Bibliography.

23

The jury took half an hour to return a guilty verdict on all three men; when the news was relayed outside, the cheers of the crowd echoed back into the court room.

There remained the mystery of how the murders were committed. When revealing this in their final confessions, Bishop and Williams had some piquant news for the world. The boy victim had *not* been Italian after all, but a Lincolnshire lad whom they had spotted as he drove cattle to Smithfield market. Among the four other victims admitted were two other boys, but they had not been Italian either. All of them had been 'hocussed and burked', the murderers revealed, by being made practically insensible with rum and laudanum, then being taken out to a water-butt, sunk like a well in Bishop's garden, and having their heads held under until they stopped struggling.

While making these horrific confessions Bishop and Williams exonerated May of any involvement in the murders; after strong representations from clergymen and others, but against the will of the judges, the Home Secretary commuted his sentence to that of transportation for life.

At 8 a.m. on Monday 5 December 1831, Bishop and Williams were hanged outside Newgate, near the Fortune of War and Smithfield Market, with the public literally clinging to chimney-pots to witness the event. Barriers collapsed, and nearby St Bartholomew's Hospital received a stream of seriously injured people. The theatre of anatomy in Windmill Street was given Williams's body for dissection and anatomization, while King's College, ironically, was presented with Bishop's.

It had been a long time, declared the *Morning Chronicle*, since King's had seen such a healthy and muscular body: 'The *deltoides* were splendidly developed and symmetrically beautiful. The *byceps* were also fully developed, and the *pectorales*, major and minor, were particularly displayed.' But the report was not intended to be sarcastic or cynical. There was great popular interest in the subject at the time, and it was not just the muscles which enthralled.

> The Phrenologist will expect from us some account of the peculiar developments that presented on an examination of the organs of the head. The organ of destructiveness was not developed but that of amativeness [propensity towards love or sexuality] was particularly full. The organ of philogenitiveness [love of, or inclination to produce, offspring] was not developed at all; but he had got ideality, and no reflection.

2

NEW POLICE *v.* OLD

AT THE FINAL TRIAL held for a bodysnatching murder, before legislation finally put paid to such activities, the prosecuting counsel stated: 'Until Lea, the officer, lent his assistance the enquiry was not efficiently pursued.' Lea was not a member of the New Police but of the 'Old'—a Runner attached to the Lambeth Street Police office. Like those in the other police offices, the Lambeth Street magistrates had retained the services of their own police, who acted not only independently of the New Police but often in fierce competition with them. What these magistrates' men enjoyed most was to uncover evidence which the bumbling New Police had overlooked. In this, they had the advantage of working under the direct control of the men who would accept or reject their evidence, and who were also fighting to retain their own power.

In the case referred to above, a young woman from Bethnal Green had complained that until she applied to Lambeth Street Police office she had received no response when she tried to interest police in the fact that her grandmother was missing. The pipe-smoking 84-year-old had not been seen for several weeks—ever since, in fact, she had gone to lodge with Edward Cook, a nightwatchman or 'Charlie' put out of business by the advent of the New Police, and his common-law wife, Eliza Ross—both of whom were rumoured to be bodysnatchers. (But then, so were a great many other people at the time.) 'Lea of Lambeth' tried, but failed, to find the old lady's body (even having another one dug up in the process), so set about gathering some circumstantial evidence. This proved to be quite flimsy, but he none the less arrested Cook, Ross, and their 12-year-old son, Ned.

The Runner, on hearing that Ned had been regaling fellow inmates in the House of Correction with hair-raising tales about the alleged murder, took a statement from the boy—with the assistance of the headmaster and headmistress of his parochial school. In it, Ned described in detail how his mother had smothered the old lady. Eliza Ross was hanged, but the affair caused public disquiet, particularly since Cook, who was acquitted, continued to swear that the boy's story was a complete fabrication.

Runners (this time from Hatton Garden police office) again became involved in the next big murder case and, initially at least, managed to extract a great deal of favourable publicity from it, despite the fact that the investigation was being handled by Superintendent Dixon of the G Division. Lea of Lambeth also poked his nose in, even though the crime occurred out of his district, in Clerkenwell.

Early one Sunday morning, in December 1832, Mr Henry Camp Shepherd, a clerk employed by a soap manufacturer just off Goswell Road, had been found murdered in the firm's counting house. As *The Times* charmingly put it: 'His skull was fractured most frightfully and his blood and brains strewed about in all directions.' Nearby was what appeared to be the weapon, a poker with blood and hair sticking to it, and an unopened safe for which the 63-year-old bachelor victim was carrying the keys. Several days later, *The Times* was reporting that 'Lloyd, the officer of Hatton Garden . . . has been persevering in his endeavours, and has spared neither expense nor trouble to trace out and bring the guilty parties to justice.'

Lloyd, another of the remaining Runners, had received information that the victim had previously complained that, while out calling on customers in 'Hampstead, Highgate and other country places' on the previous Friday, he had been followed by some low and suspicious-looking fellows 'having the appearance of glaziers'. Lloyd immediately sped out in that direction, but failed to trace the men. However, after enquiring locally he had heard (said *The Times*) that two men answering the description had been seen lurking about the neighbourhood of the soap firm. 'But, unfortunately, their identity cannot be sufficiently ascertained to assist the officers.'

This sounds like a bit of humbug, to which, as Charles Dickens was later to observe, the Runners were much addicted. He found them men of indifferent character, puffed up by incompetent magistrates anxious to conceal their own deficiencies, and too much in the habit of consorting with thieves. 'They never lost a chance of jobbing and trading in mystery and making the most of themselves'. The penny-a-liners, with whom, he noticed, they were hand in glove, were only too happy to assist in this.

As with the previous case, the Runners acquired their most vital information from inside a prison where an inmate had purportedly been overheard boastfully claiming that the Shepherd murder was the work of his two pals, Tom Ainsley and Jem Martin. The unfortunate pair were promptly arrested and taken before Mr Allen Laing of Hatton Garden, said to be the model for Dickens's dreadful example of magisterial arrogance and ineptitude, Mr Fang in *Oliver Twist*. He held several 'examinations' of the suspects—all of them in private. Ainsley was released but Martin remanded in custody. Whilst so incarcerated, *The Times* reported, Lea visited the suspect to inspect his clothing and found it 'bloodstained'. 'It did not, it appears, occur to the Hatton Garden Officers or the constable of police who apprehended him to examine his clothes.' Lea also discovered that, while in prison, Martin had got rid of a bloodstained handkerchief by burning. He took note of the man's alibis 'which', declared the *Times* reporter confidently, 'he will be able to prove by witnesses on the next examination to be false'.

What in fact happened on Martin's final examination, after he had spent a fortnight in custody, was that he was quietly discharged 'free from imputation . . . there being no evidence to present against him'. Despite further (less well-advertised) efforts by the New Police, the murderer of Mr Shepherd was never found.

The Runners were, of course, not without skills, and had considerable experience in detective work as well as Press manipulation. They could also move about more freely than the New Police, and had the advantage of operating incognito. The question of whether there ought to be any permanent plain-clothes officers in the New Police was to be given a thorough airing during 1833—in the wake of the Sergeant Popay affair.

P S Popay had obtained information on a forthcoming forbidden meeting in Coldbath Fields, Clerkenwell, by posing as a poor artist and infiltrating himself into the National Union of the Working Classes. The commissioners reacted to the news of this working-class defiance with a fine show of force and a riot ensued, during which a P C Culley was knifed to death. At the inquest, the jury insisted on bringing in a verdict of 'justifiable homicide'. (Superintendent Thomas came in for allegations of high-handedness during the riot from the principal anti-police witness but defended himself by claiming that, at the time, he had been upset by the death of P C Culley.)

Enquiries were demanded into both matters: Popay's 'spying' and what had caused the Coldbath Fields riot to develop. Select Committees condemned the employment of 'police spies' as abhorrent to the feelings of the people and alien to the spirit of the Constitution. (It was around this time that the high-profile Vidocq was instrumental in foiling a Parisian revolt, which cannot have helped.) Subsequently, Sergeant Popay was dismissed for his over-enthusiasm and the commissioners exonerated of blame for the riot. The classic solution.

Another parliamentary committee discussed the organization of the New Police and compared their performance with the 'old' variety. To it, Lambeth Magistrate Mr John Hardwick ventured the opinion that 'the Metropolitan Police are efficient in the preventive part of their duties. In the detective part they are, and ever will be, deficient — from the nature of their regulations and their discipline.'

This statement probably pleased the middle-aged ex-soldier Commissioner Rowan, since he was a great believer in stern discipline and considered prevention the chief role of the New Police. But his younger colleague, the ex-lawyer Richard Mayne, wanted them to be all-rounders. When asked what the Metropolitan Police could do about their weakness in this area, Mr Hardwick suggested they pick out their most intelligent men, put them in plain clothes, and train and employ them as a detective branch. But the very idea of plain-clothes police was still anathema, and that year, unfortunately, the Metropolitan Police also lost the man who had conducted their most successful case to date when Superintendent Thomas became the deputy chief constable of Manchester City Police.

However, by the end of 1835 the New Police did at least have a sympathetic Home Secretary in Lord John Russell. Other Whig Home Secretaries, who had followed Sir Robert Peel, had been at best half-hearted in their dealings with the New Police, which they regarded as a Tory invention. One of them, Lord Duncannon, had been a close friend of their arch-enemy, Bow Street magistrate Sir Frederick Roe, and had allowed a great deal of interference from the still powerful magistrates. But in 1835 Lord John Russell got the job. He had been with Peel on an 1827 Parliamentary Select Committee which had declared that the art of crime had increased faster than the art of detection. Lord John believed in the need for the New Police, who, as 1836 drew to a close, had another sensational case on which to practise their embryonic powers of detection.

On the afternoon of 28 December, 1836, PC Pegler of the S or Hampstead Division was patrolling the east side of Edgware Road when horrified cries of 'Police! Police!' induced him to cross over to the west side and so to the adjacent T or Kensington Division. A distraught working man, showed him a parcel which he had spotted tucked behind an up-ended flagstone. Inside was a nude female torso, the arms still attached, but minus the head and legs.

There were no markings on the sacking which had been wrapped round the trunk, but Pegler was a meticulous policeman and, having procured a wheelbarrow and taken the remains to a workhouse, he examined the inside of the now empty sack where he found some mahogany shavings. He also retrieved a scrap of patched nankeen cotton found lying near the bag. P C Pegler was also prepared to indulge in a little deduction, suggesting that, since it had been snowing since Christmas Day and snow had built up around the sack but there was none beneath it, it must have been deposited there before that time. He was seconded to T Division to assist Inspector Feltham with the enquiry. Surgeons told them that the trunk was that of a woman between 40 and 50 years of age, and that she had 'an unusual interior malformation'. But they did not get much further until, ten days later, a head was found — seven miles away in the Regent's Canal at Stepney. The trunk was disinterred and found to fit the head. In the seemingly vain hope of someone recognizing the features, despite their being bloated, battered, and bruised and with one eye almost knocked out, the head was placed into spirit and put on public show in the workhouse.

The canal actually crosses the northern end of Edgware Road before going on to Stepney, so it was quite reasonable to deduce that the head might have been placed in it at that point, been caught up on a barge, and carried down to where it was found. Maybe the legs had also been dropped in? The canal was dragged for several days in the hope of finding them — but to no avail. The legs *were* found eventually, but in quite a different part of London — in the Camberwell marshes, seven miles southeast of Edgware Road. The legs had also been wrapped in hessian, but this time the cloth bore some markings which enabled police to trace it back to a man who, three years earlier, had used the original sack to send his potatoes to Covent Garden. But follow-up enquiries proved unproductive. Feltham and Pegler were stymied once more.

Ten weeks after the trunk was found, a Mr Gay came forward to say that the victim might be his sister, Hannah Brown, who had gone missing just before Christmas. He could not swear that the head was hers but thought it possible, since it had a damaged ear, as did his sister since a fellow-servant had pulled out her earring. Hannah, it transpired, had been engaged to a Mr Greenacre, currently living in Camberwell but claiming to have an estate in America where he was to take his bride. Mr Gay had not met Greenacre, but had twice glimpsed him waiting for his sister. They had planned to marry on Christmas Day; Hannah was to stay with a friend the night before, but she had never arrived. Later on Christmas Eve,

(*Left*) The founding father of Scotland Yard's first Detective Branch, ex-lawyer Richard Mayne, in 1835, when he was 38 years old. By then he had served for five years as one of the first two Metropolitan police commissioners. (Courtesy of the Metropolitan Police)

(*Below*) Frontispiece of an 1837 bestseller on the murder of Hannah Brown by James Greenacre. (Courtesy of the British Museum)

The Body of HANNAH BROWN as Mangled by GREENACRE, her intended HUSBAND.

THE
PADDINGTON TRAGEDY

A
CIRCUMSTANTIAL NARRATIVE
OF THE
LIVES AND TRIAL
OF
JAMES GREENACRE
AND
THE WOMAN GALE,
FOR THE MURDER OF
MRS. HANNAH BROWN,
HIS INTENDED WIFE,
WHICH WAS BROUGHT TO LIGHT
BY THE
DISCOVERY OF HER
MUTILATED REMAINS;
HIS ATTEMPT AT SUICIDE;
EXAMINATION AND CONFESSION.

THE WHOLE COLLECTED FROM
PRIVATE AND AUTHENTIC SOURCES.

LONDON:
ORLANDO HODGSON, 111, FLEET STREET.

Inspector Aggs as a reward from the fund for good conduct', wrote Mayne. Runners never had problems like this—but then they had the sense to arrest and charge *someone*, even it they didn't have sufficient evidence, which at least took the heat out of the situation.

All of Inspector Aggs's dashing about proved to be in vain; but there was more to come in later years, as he followed up 'confessions' and further sightings of the suspect which even led him, in 1842, to the island of Jersey. The case took on yet another lease of life in 1848, when a young man called in to tell Inspector Tedman of D Division that, at the time of the murder, he had been a servant in a house not far from the pub, to which a frequent visitor had been a man named Holland, a brother of the house-keeper. The other servants had felt that the man's clothes so resembled those described as worn by the suspect that, to prevent his capture, they held a collection which raised sufficient money for him to buy either a new hat or a pair of trousers. Holland, it seemed, was always out and about early in the morning, and was also an occasional customer at the Kings Arms.

This information received some publicity which brought forth some more information. A young man named Gee claimed to have seen a man run out of the pub at 6 a.m. on the fateful morning, pausing only to stoop over a gutter to wash blood from his hands. Gee had told his master at the time and he had passed on the intelligence to Mr Rawlinson, a magistrate at Marylebone Lane police office,[1] but he had 'treated the matter rather lightly'. On reading about this in the newspapers, the now retired Inspector Aggs got in touch and admitted that this evidence about the running man had been passed on to him, but that he had paid little attention to it at the time.

Tedman worked hard, and spent his own money, tracking Holland to Southampton, but informed the commissioners he could not afford to pay Gee's fare down there to have him identified. They paid up, but Gee proved uncertain whether Holland was the man he had seen that day, and no further action was taken.

WHILE THE PRESS were charting the progress of the Italian Boy enquiry in 1831, they also kept up a running commentary on the deadly progress of 'the Asiatic Cholera'. Originally from India, where it was endemic, the disease had killed 5,000 in St Petersburg before traversing the rest of Europe and landing at Sunderland. By the time Bishop and

---

[1] Opened in 1821 to cope with the growing population north of Oxford Street.

Williams were hanged, 102 people had died, and there were the beginnings of a countrywide panic.

When a suspected case in Newcastle upon Tyne turned out to be a false alarm, everyone breathed a sigh of relief. But the respite was brief. By August 1832 cholera had invaded the south and was cutting a swathe through London's poorer districts, killing more than a dozen Metropolitan Police officers that year, mainly from the Thameside divisions.

The E and F divisions lost two P Cs, a sergeant and a superintendent, but one E or Holborn Division sergeant who managed to escape the scourge was Charles Frederick Field, the son of a Chelsea publican.

At 5ft. 10in. he was quite a tall man for his day, and his imposing presence, ebullience, and confidence had led him to spend most of his youth attempting to succeed as an actor in London's unlicensed theatres. But the going was hard, and when the New Police were launched in 1829 Field was among the first applicants. He was taken on as a sergeant and sent to the slum-ridden E Division, which at that time abutted the northern border of the Metropolitan Police district.

According to a later memoir on Field in the *Illustrated Times*, he scored a great success on his first night out, in St Giles's High Street, 'on one of those "raw and gusty eves" in November, "whereon the very wind did grieve"':

> An Irish row occurred in the neighbourhood of those fearful sinks of villainy and iniquity called Buckeridge Street and Rats' Castle, which ended in the capture of a notorious highway robber; and thus, on his *first* night, he was enabled to make his *"first* charge". Fortune, fickle creature, smiled on Field, and ever since has continued to pour down upon him her bounteous gifts.

By the following year Frederick Field had been promoted to inspector and transferred to the L or Lambeth Division which, with its numerous brothels and thieves' haunts, was scarcely more salubrious than the E. Despite being south of the river, Lambeth's populace was well placed to prey upon the well-to-do — thanks to the splendid new Waterloo Bridge, with its Doric columns and elliptical arches, which led almost directly into the glamorous theatreland of the Strand and the Aldwych.

It was in a house close by Waterloo Bridge that, on the morning of 26 May 1838, Inspector Field took charge of the enquiry into the sudden death of 'the Countess' — a very beautiful 28-year-old prostitute named Eliza Grimwood.

Dr Cooke, the surgeon who examined the body, declared that Eliza had committed suicide by cutting her own throat — almost decapitating herself in the process. Field, now 33 years old, with almost nine years' service in hard stations, arrived after the doctor left, and did not agree with this diagnosis. He asked Cooke to come back and take another look. Eliza, he pointed out, also had a deep cut across the *back* of her neck and defensive cuts to her hands which she could hardly have made herself. The doctor had to agree that this did look suspicious, and decided that, after all, the 'remarkably handsome' Eliza must have been murdered.

Eliza was one of the Lambeth inhabitants who put the Waterloo Bridge to good use. She would cross over to the Strand theatres, resplendent in her pale brown dress and blue silk bonnet with a flower on it, and with a feather boa draped around her neck, to pick up clients whom she brought back across the river to her lodgings at 12 Wellington Terrace. She had done this the night before her body had been discovered, Field learned, returning with a tall, well-dressed man of gentlemanly appearance. But the young maidservant who let them in could not describe him any further, the night being dark and she not having taken a candle to the door.

Field noticed that there were two dents in the pillow of Eliza's bed but, unlike some of his predecessors, he refrained from rushing off in pursuit of a shadowy suspect. First, he made a thorough search of the rest of the house, starting with the bedroom of William Hubbard, a bricklayer and Eliza's live-in lover whom, from the tone of his subsequent reports, Field instantly suspected.

It was Hubbard who had discovered the body early in the morning when coming down from his attic room which he occupied alone when Eliza had company. His story was that he had been passing the back parlour-cum-bedroom where she took her clients when, near the open door, he saw a bundle of clothes. Then he spotted a candle from Eliza's candlestick lying on the hall mat near the street door. He went into Eliza's room, which he found awash with her blood.

On dashing upstairs to one of the lodgers' rooms, he found the occupant, Miss Glover, had a man friend with her, so withdrew and went to tell the servant instead. She promptly had hysterics. He went back to Miss Glover's room, knocked on the door, and told them what had happened — oddly formal behaviour in such a house at such a time of crisis. Then he fetched the surgeon, and someone (there was to be much discussion as to whom) sounded the alarm outside which brought P C Charles Burgess Goff from his beat in Waterloo Road.

The main item missing from Eliza's room (apart from the chamber-pot, which was later found in the kitchen) was the murder weapon. Field took Hubbard's room apart but found nothing except three or four 'bloodstains' on the undersheet which did not appear fresh. But between the sheets were several membership cards, one of which had blood on both sides. He also took charge of Hubbard's corduroy trousers, which were marked with several small 'bloodstains'. In later years, when describing the case to Charles Dickens, Field gave the impression (or the author misunderstood) that the pair of gloves he found under Eliza's pillow were taken instantly to the Union Hall magistrates, who instructed him to track down the owner immediately and diligently. This he did, but (according to his own and contemporary newspaper reports) not until three weeks later. What his tale does show, however, is that the New Police were continuing to consult the magistrates on the conduct of their investigations.

On the day after the murder Field did take off in pursuit of Eliza's gentle-man caller, leaving P C Goff in charge of the house — with strict instructions to keep an eye on Hubbard.

One of the things which strike one most when looking back on these early investigations is the amount of dashing about the officer in charge of the case was obliged to do. These days, he stays put most of the time and every-one dashes around him; only in detective fiction does he continue to do all his own grass-roots enquiries. Not so in 1838. This was partly due to the smallness of the teams allotted to an enquiry, and also to the lack of a rapid means of communication to transfer information back to the man at the heart of the investigation. Nowadays, of course, the answers to many questions can be acquired quickly by telephone, telex, radio, or fax machine, and these aids then enable instant use to be made of any intelligence so received. The first detectives had only the post, messengers, and the 'route paper' system. Well aware of the importance of rapid communications, the commissioners organized a system whereby information on recent crimes, stolen property, and wanted men was taken to a division by mounted courier. That division passed it on to the next, adding its own intelli-gence, and so on — but it could be of only limited help in a complex enquiry.

Neither did the police have the easy mobility of today. There was no police transport, so they had to rely on the public variety — which was not only limited and expensive but had to be paid for out of the investigators' own pockets and then claimed back from (as we have seen) often reluctant commissioners at the end of the enquiry. But, of course, if the transport of the detectives was limited, so was that of the suspects, particularly if they were poor.

In addition, suspects, by their speech, dress and manner, quickly divided themselves into gentlemen and ladies and others. If the suspect was a gentleman or lady, the field was narrowed considerably. 'Others' tended to subdivide themselves conveniently by dressing according to their trade. Many did not have even one change of clothes with which to disguise themselves — so that clothing formed an important means of identification.

Another advantage was that London was very much smaller than it is now. Thus, when Field 'went and traced out the cabman who had brought the deceased home from the Strand Theatre', it was much simpler than it would be at present. The same cabs plied a limited area nightly, and the cabmen also tended to remember crossing the Waterloo Bridge, where they had to pay the much-resented two-penny toll.

And, indeed, one of the drivers did remember being hailed on the night in question by a female and a man, 'very much a gentleman in appearance', between the Strand Theatre and St Clement Danes Church and taking them to Wellington Terrace. But he could not recall much more about the man, other than that he was a little taller than his own 5ft. 6in., swarthy, with very large dark whiskers but no moustachios.

A musician on his way home from his evening's stint with the Covent Garden Theatre orchestra remembered seeing such a man as had been described by the cabby, entering 12 Wellington Terrace with a female at 12.15 a.m. John Sharp, a newspaper reporter, recalled hearing 'an unfortunate woman' saying 'He is here' to her friend in the Strand Theatre that Friday night — 'By which I concluded she alluded to some male in the pit' — then saw her go off to join the man. He identified Eliza's body as that of the same 'unfortunate woman'.

Field gathered these witnesses, and the surgeons (who had even more reason to believe she had been murdered when they discovered that Eliza had also been stabbed in the chest and stomach through her stays) for the opening of the inquest on Monday. He was obliged to waste a vital day there, and another on the following Thursday, when the jury sat for eleven hours without reaching a conclusion. Despite this, they gave permission for burial the following day (as Eliza's body was fast decomposing).

In between, and at the end of the long inquest days, Field was never still. He searched the forty 'dry arches' under the Waterloo Road and Bridge, drained the cesspool at 12 Wellington Terrace, and peered up the chimneys. He had the water pipes taken down and the fields opposite combed. The houses of Hubbard's relatives received similar treatment but no suitable weapon was found. P C Goff did find a penknife under floorboards of 12 Wellington Terrace.

Field also went to 'places of public resort of foreigners' such as hotels, gambling houses, and the Opera, and made enquiries at the Passport Office, docks, and wharves as to whether a swarthy foreigner had left by one of the steamboats — but Hubbard was always kept very much in view. He discovered that the bricklayer lover had been violent not only to his estranged wife but to Eliza (who was his first cousin) as well; had been very jealous of her, especially with regard to one particular customer with whom she intended to go to the Epsom Races; and had even threatened to 'do them both in'. To cap it all, he had been seen around the Waterloo Road area early in the morning before the discovery of the murder.

All very promising; but the water was quickly being muddied by inquest witnesses who contradicted not only each other but themselves as well. Some of them were probably lying for the reward money or out of fear of Hubbard, and one was clearly mad. As always in such cases, time was wasted following up information from anonymous letters, while the convoluted and ultimately dead-end clue of the pair of gloves also frittered away three more days.

It is obvious that Field had the right ideas about building up a case against a suspect while keeping his options open as far as others were concerned. On the other hand, it is true to say that some of his enquiries had been directed by the coroner and some in consultation with the Union Hall magistrates. In fact, at the end of the first day of the inquest, Field had enquired of the coroner whether he should take Hubbard into custody — which must have galled Mayne. The coroner replied that the police must follow what course they thought proper, but that he would make no order since he did not think there was enough evidence. The magistrates did not think so either when Field, fearing Hubbard was about to abscond, arrested him and took him before them. He was discharged.

Hubbard was never arrested again for the murder and neither was anyone else — despite a six-week enquiry. Apart from inquest days it had been interrupted for Field only by a day off 'for duty at the Review'[2] on 9 July and, probably (there being a gap at this point in his carefully kept official résumé of the case), four days for duty at Queen Victoria's Coronation on 28 June. At that time, writes Elizabeth Longford in *Victoria R I*,

---

[2] By the new Queen, Victoria, of her troops in Hyde Park.

'the town was all a mob, the park an encampment'. The New Police had more to worry about than an unfortunate woman named Eliza Grimwood.

By the middle of 1839, Lord John Russell was busy seeing that the provinces got the benefit of something similar to the Metropolitan Police and introducing his two Police Bills for 'improving the police in and near the Metropolis'. This was to be achieved by enlarging the area covered by the Metropolitan Police, incorporating the Thames Police and Bow Street Horse Patrol, curtailing the powers of the magistrates to purely judicial ones, and the final disbanding of their 'officers' or Runners. The New Police had won.

3

ENTER PEARCE

ANY ACCOMPLICE who had not actually committed the murder of Mr Robert Westwood would be pardoned if he came forward and pointed the finger at the one who did, announced Lord John Russell in June 1839. This was standard procedure in a murder enquiry which was getting nowhere. But the Westwood murder, another of the high-profile, difficult-to-solve variety, could not have come at a worse moment than when Russell was pushing his new Police Acts through Parliament.

The victim, 55-year-old Robert Westwood, was a watchmaker and the inventor of 'the celebrated eight-day watch'. In those days the mere owning of a watch indicated a person of some substance, and one could be risking one's very life carrying it about. Mr Westwood had dozens on his premises, many of them extremely valuable. The bedrooms were above the shop at 35 Princes Street, in Soho, but fear of burglary caused Westwood to sleep in a back room of the ground floor instead — only after he had made sure his doors were double-bolted, locked, and chained. Despite all his security precautions, at just after midnight on Monday, 3 June 1839, Robert Westwood was battered about the head, his throat slashed, and his clothing set on fire. No one was sure in what order these ferocious attacks occurred, but surgeons later agreed that any could have killed him.

The police of C Division were on the scene remarkably quickly — in time, indeed, to extinguish the flames. Neither was there to be any difficulty in finding suspects. Quite the reverse, in fact.

Firstly — since there were no signs of forced entry — there were the other occupants of the house. The elderly Mrs Westwood (at least 20 years older than her husband) had, she said, first become aware something might be wrong when, at about 11.30 p.m., she heard scuffling downstairs. She had decided it was merely her husband putting out the cat. Fifteen minutes later she heard someone go out, closing the front door behind them. Only after she began to smell smoke and heard the occasional groan from the floor below did she go upstairs to fetch their new young maid and Mr

Gerard, their elderly and deaf lodger, telling them she was sure her husband had been murdered.

The billowing smoke prevented them getting into Mr Westwood's room so they opened the front door and shouted for the police. A passer-by fetched P C Timothy Gimlet. His rattle summoned two more, and, with the aid of those other classic police-report figures, 'bystanders', they managed to put out the fire before the brigade arrived. 'There is a body in here,' one of the bystanders pointed out, causing P C Thomas Chilman to get down on his hands and knees and feel around in the smoke. He soon located a pair of feet and legs, a great deal of blood, and many feathers. Near the body was a heavy sash-window weight with hairs stuck to it; but later, when P C Chilman presented this in court as a possible weapon, he was forced to admit that there was no way of telling whether the hair was animal or human.

The first senior officers to arrive from Vine Street station house were Superintendent Thomas Baker and Inspector John Jervis. The latter certainly looked the part, being nearly 6 ft. tall; but, although he had almost ten years' experience, he had been an inspector for less than a year.

Jervis searched for further weapons, and in a drawer found a knife which looked as though it had been recently wiped of blood. He also surveyed the scene and decided that there was no way in which anyone could get in through the back and no place where anyone could conceal themselves to lie in wait, after having entered before closing time. Mrs Westwood disagreed, insisting there were many such hiding-places about the house.

At first it was unclear whether anything had been stolen; but when Westwood's foreman, Charles Louis Serouche, arrived that afternoon he revealed that over 80 of the most valuable timepieces were missing, including several of Westwood's patent eight-day watches, some made of gold. Moreover, it was evident that whoever had committed the crime knew the most valuable pieces and where they were kept. Messengers were sent galloping off with route papers containing details of the stolen property. The foreman himself was suspect, of course, particularly since he had lived on the premises until a recent disagreement with Mr Westwood. Having disagreements with Mr Westwood was not uncommon, the police were soon to discover.

At 8 p.m. in the evening following the murder, the inquest was opened in the upper room of the nearby Plough public house—only to be hastily adjourned and transferred to the chapel of St James's workhouse after fears were voiced that the pub's floor might collapse under the weight of the onlookers. All the members of the inquest jury were close neighbours of Westwood. Eight of them lived in Princes Street itself, which, given the man's irascible reputation, must surely have qualified them as possible suspects.

The elderly Mrs Westwood pointed her accusing finger, not at a neighbour, but at William and Caroline Stevenson, who until recently had also lodged with them, and who had, she claimed, threatened to 'do for' her husband only ten days earlier, after Westwood had asked them, and Caroline's sister, to leave. The cause of the trouble had been domestic strife between the Stevensons and the number and assortment of Mrs Stevenson's visitors, of whom Westwood disapproved. They were said to be admirers, although this was denied by Mrs Stevenson, who claimed they came to see her unmarried sister. Serouche, the foreman, seems to have done some mischief-making here, informing Westwood that he had seen Mrs Stevenson getting out of a cab 'without a bonnet' after having been out all night, and that he had seen some of her woman friends entering a brothel.

It was all too much for Mrs Stevenson, who, instead of taking other lodgings with her husband, had run off home to her mother — taking with her the keys to 35 Princes Street. She still had them when the inquest opened. When questioned, she claimed that she did not know she had the keys until her mother came across them in her belongings, and that they had never been out of her hands since. She was said by her husband to have become suicidal owing to the blackening of her character by Westwood and, consequently, Mrs Westwood claimed, Stevenson had threatened Westwood's life.

It was not only the proliferation of lodgers past and present which muddied the waters of many of those early police enquiries. The high incidence of live-in servants had a similar effect. Both groups made promising potential suspects, since they had the opportunity to commit the crime and access to and knowledge of the premises and its occupants — not to mention having motives brought on by poverty and close-quarters living. But even when completely innocent they could make doubtful witnesses, since they had their job or home to protect.

The last person to have seen Mr Westwood alive was the new servant, Maria Pritty. She had been responsible for the final locking-up after she let the lodger in at 11 p.m. on the fateful night. She told police that she had gained the impression that the ex-lodger, Mr Stevenson, and Westwood were on good terms. But then came the revelation that she had been almost fully dressed when the police arrived, and had been seen talking to some men while the others were trying to put out the fire.

Then a neighbour came forward and told the police he had seen two middle-aged, lower-class men, dressed in dark frock coats, emerging from 35 Princes Street at about 12.30 a.m. on the night of the murder. He thought he knew one of them, but the man had avoided his eye. One of those helpful passers-by, a young man named George Robinson, had worn a frock coat and, said the witness, answered to the description of one of the suspects. Robinson was called upon to to say just what he had been doing in Princes Street at that hour, how he supported himself, and how he came by a wound on his cheek. Neither the coroner nor the jury were happy with his replies, in which he contradicted himself and other witnesses. The wound, he claimed, was a burn from when he helped put out the fire; but one of the surgeons, in court to give evidence about the body, said it looked more like a graze to him.

The coroner and his jury pondered long on whether Robinson should be taken into custody, but finally decided that he should be handed over to C Division's more experienced Inspector Beresford, who had held the rank for six years. He would examine Robinson's lodgings, make further enquiries, then decide whether to detain the man. Beresford let him go, saying he could find no evidence against him. It was true that Robinson was in possession of Mr Westwood's hat, but that, he said, he had picked up in mistake for his own in the hurry when the police pushed him out, and he had made no secret of the fact.

The Times made it plain that it favoured *Mrs* Westwood as a suspect, or at least as an accomplice. It was not that long ago, it pointed out, that she had had to appeal to Marlborough Street magistrates to restrain her husband's violence towards her. Did it not, moreover, seem odd that she pleaded ignorance of some anonymous threatening letters Westwood had received when he had told so many other people about them? But, as the newspaper had to admit, Mr Westwood was a man of 'extremely irritable temper' and 'rather peculiar habits'—particularly with dissatisfied customers. One sea captain had had the watch he complained about snatched out of his hand, thrown on the floor, and stamped on, and a young man found himself facing a pistol and a threat to blow his brains out if he didn't leave at once. On the penultimate day of the inquest, one of the jury in fact joined the burgeoning ranks of the suspects. He also, it transpired, had once lived at 35 Princes Street as Westwood's foreman 'but had lately opposed him in business' and, it was alleged, threatened his life.[1]

The jury brought in a verdict of murder by a person or persons unknown, and congratulated Superintendent Baker and Inspectors Beresford and Jervis on their zeal, promptness and efficiency, and 'for their efforts (tho' unsuccessful) to discover the diabolical perpetrators'. The Press had, unfortunately, already left when these bouquets were handed out, Superintendent Baker informed the commissioners when he sent them notes of the inquest. Their response was to send in Inspector Nicholas Pearce from Scotland Yard to 'manage' the case. Sergeant Charles Otway, also of A Division was (according to the Press) already assisting.

Pearce, another six-footer, who had been a member of the 66-strong Bow Street Foot Patrol, had joined the New Police as a sergeant in February 1830 and went straight to the newly-formed H Division in the East End dockland area. Despite an early transfer to the more glamorous A or Whitehall Division, within ten months he had resigned. Four months later he was back again — at the same rank — and, after 18 months, he was made inspector. This chopping and changing was by no means unusual in those difficult early days, and did not necessarily prevent men from getting on in the New Police, which needed good experienced men but could not offer them very high wages — only the possibility of advancement.

According to Douglas G. Browne, in *The Rise of Scotland Yard*, it appeared that Pearce became one of the four special mobile inspectors operating from Scotland Yard and nominally attached to A Division, who, at least as early as 1840, were entrusted with the duty of watching the activities of London's habitual criminals — 'and he [Pearce] was further given a roving commission as investigator in certain cases of murder of other serious crimes in the Metropolis.'

The list of possible suspects in the Westwood case continued to lengthen. As inside knowledge was a strong factor, Pearce had a list drawn up of all those who had worked for Mr Westwood. There were sixteen in all: engravers, finishers, gilders, and makers of dials, escapements, motions, and hands — there was even a 'secret springer' — and all had addresses in or near the watch- and clockmakers' district of Clerkenwell.

Having no luck there, and faced with such a confusion of suspects, Inspector Pearce tried another tack — tracing the stolen watches. He

---

[1] Anonymous letter quoted in *The Times*, 10 June 1839

already had a reputation for tenacity when chasing a suspect, and soon had Beresford at it as well, sending him off to make enquiries at pawnbrokers, jewellers, and watchmakers at Gravesend, following up some information received. Beresford wrote from Chatham: he had had no luck at Gravesend, but would go to Maidstone the next day, Friday, and return to Chatham in the evening. If he had not received further instructions by post he would return to London on Saturday.

Pearce must have been out in pursuit as well, because Mr Yardley, the chief clerk, added a marginal note to the letter: 'Mr May[2] — as Inspector Pearce is managing this case obtain directions from the Commissioners for the guidance of Inspector Beresford.' Beresford was thus 'guided' to Broadstairs from where a boat had been reported stolen — possibly by some suspects, said to have been seen in the area, so that they could escape across the Channel. This meant the inspector taking the first stage-coach to Ramsgate on Saturday, then travelling on to Broadstairs the following day. By the time he arrived the boat owner already had his vessel back, having been across to Boulogne to retrieve it from the French police, who had picked up the thief. Beresford crossed over to Boulogne, arriving there late on Tuesday evening, 'being obliged to go round by Dover there being no steamboat direct from Ramsgate'. It transpired that the boat thief, who by now had been taken to the Belgian border and set free, was a Prussian trying to get back home, and Beresford, who had seen copies of his papers, felt sure he had nothing to do with the murder of Mr Westwood. Another wild goose chase.

Digging even further back into Westwood's past produced yet another possible suspect and, in Pearce's eyes, a very likely one, as he made plain in a report to the commissioners dated 22 June 1839. William Campion had been sacked by Westwood four years previously, was known to be of bad character, and, as Pearce pointed out, had worked abroad at one time in Paris and Holland, so would be knowledgeable about the foreign markets for stolen goods. Campion could not now get a job and was destitute, due, he had told an acquaintance, to Mr Westwood refusing to 'give him a character'. He had been heard to say that 'some day he'd be damned if he did not cut his b— throat'.

Another watchmaker informed Campion that the police were enquiring about him, and advised him to go and see them. He replied that he had intended to go to see Mrs Westwood when he had heard about the murder,

<hr />

[2] John May, superintendent of A Division.

but that his clothes were in such a state he was too ashamed; then he had left quickly, refusing to give his address. Pearce and Otway took this watchmaker, and another who knew Campion, in search of the suspect 'until 2 o'clock this morning but without finding him'. They were now worried the man was forewarned and asked 'the Commissioner's directions upon the propriety of describing[3] him'. Five days later Pearce saw Campion, and reported firmly that the man had 'not the slightest suspicion attached to him' since he now was employed, leading a regular life, and had alibis.

Right from the start the police had been aware that one group of people had even stronger motives than anyone else for murdering Westwood — the relatives and friends of a young man named William Reading who had been hanged on the watchmaker's evidence. Twice during his 30 years in business Westwood had been robbed in a manner which may have helped sour his nature. On the first occasion, soon after he commenced trading, three men broke in, tied him to a bedpost, and stole a number of valuable pieces. The second time was in August 1822, while he and his wife were at church. The culprits, using false keys, had made off with 44 gold sovereigns, watches, and jewellery, worth around £2,000. A witness claimed to have seen William Reading loitering with four others in the churchyard next to the shop, 'talking earnestly', and looking at Westwood's premises. When apprehended by Marlborough Street Runners, Reading had six sovereigns on him, two of which the watchmaker firmly and unequivocally identified as his property since they bore his special mark. That evidence, plus a letter said to have been found on the prisoner asking his brother to get rid of certain items, was enough to hang the young man. Ironically, by the time of Westwood's murder 17 years later, he would not have suffered such a fate, as several Acts of Parliament, sponsored largely by Peel and Lord John Russell, had reduced dramatically the number of capital offences.

There was little hard evidence to back up these suspicions, but by late July, possibly in desperation, Pearce declared himself sure that Reading's relatives and friends had done the deed 'due to the considerable degree of malice used in mangling the body of their victim'. If so, they had waited a long time for revenge. One of Reading's brothers was now himself a watchmaker, in Mile End. But Pearce admitted to the commissioners that he

---

[3] Having his description circulated.

had not been able to find anything against him, despite the fact he was 'constantly watched by constables'. Neither had he been able to trace Reading's 'bosom friend', George Redgrave, 'supposed to be an old and undetected burglar'. But he had heard that he had been 'seen about a month since with new clothes on when previously very shabby'. Two other members of this 'gang' were James Harding, who kept a pub at Brighton, and Sam Cotterell, who had been charged with, but never convicted of, a similar crime. Cotterell was also said to be newly well-dressed and visiting fairs and seaports, and to be very likely to go to Goodwood Races. It appeared essential to Pearce that some person who knew them should attend Goodwood also, and for that person to go on to Brighton to enquire about Harding. 'Cotterell', he added disingenuously, 'is known to Inspector Pearce.' Pearce liked to get out and about.

The arrival of a letter from New York concerning one Nicholas William Carron soon put all other theories and suspects in the shade. Small of stature (5ft. 5in.), Carron was not new to the suspect list either, having first come into the picture eight days after the murder when Superintendent Baker had received an anonymous letter suggesting him as the prime suspect.

Every case attracted anonymous letters, and following them up usually resulted only in a waste of police time. But this letter was meatier than usual. It claimed not only that Carron, a paper-hanger who lived at 32 Princes Street (two doors from the Westwoods) knew the watchmaker's premises well, having decorated them not long before, but that he had been hard up at the time of the murder. Furthermore, Carron had 'concealed himself' all day following the murder, then left London—having shaved off his whiskers, adopted a disguise, and taken on a false name. He had been strangely agitated just before his departure, and had said he was thinking of going abroad. The fact that Carron was a paper-hanger was significant because of the discovery at the scene of the murder of the sash weight, and of a strange apron with large pockets, which had turned out to be a paper-hangers apron.

Inspector Beresford had been given the task of looking into the allegations; but (he later shamefacedly admitted) on discovering that Carron had indeed fled, he had decided that his exit had been due solely to the fact that his creditors were threatening him. Carron had left his wife and four children behind, telling them he was going to Blackheath to find work and would come back, or write, in about a week. Two children were put into St James's Workhouse, two were sent to relatives, and the wife went back to her mother. Beresford went chasing off to Chatham and Boulogne; and Carron was forgotten.

Now there was new information in a letter which Carron's relatives in London had received from a third party in New York, telling them that Carron had arrived there and that his wife was now en route to join him. Carron, the letter went on, had taken apartments and was furnishing them in preparation for her arrival. He was shortly to send for his children and recompense all parties concerned for the expense incurred. One thing was certain. Not only was Carron still nowhere to be found in this country but, hurried enquiries revealed, neither was Mrs Carron. She had left her mother about two months earlier, telling her she was going to travel in service with a French lady and would write soon — but no letter had ever arrived.

A red-faced Beresford suggested interviewing an ex-housekeeper of Carron's — a widow with three children, whom Carron had thrown out when she became pregnant by him. The inspector had known the woman in better times, when she and her husband had kept a stationer's shop just off Oxford Street. He had now traced her to a Lincolnshire workhouse, and was sure she would be co-operative. Beresford was duly sent up to Lincolnshire — and on enquiries to a great many other places 'in Town and Country' during the next few months. The ex-housekeeper duly recognized the apron and sash weight as items she'd seen about Carron's place, and described the man as a bad character who spent a great deal of time with a prostitute in Waterloo Road. (It was only a year since Eliza Grimwood's murder and there are striking similarities in the crimes, but I found no record of any connection being made.) But what they really needed to do was to trace Carron.

Pearce had already sent the reward notices to New York, but he now made a daring and unusual move. He wrote to William Cartwright, an old acquaintance now living in New York, gave him what information he had about Carron's supposed whereabouts, and asked him to make discreet enquiries. If the enquiries met with success, he told Cartwright, there would be a reward. It was a calculated risk. Cartwright was an ex-Metropolitan policeman, but one of the many who had been dismissed from the force.

There was no reply. Early in 1840 Pearce wrote again, and yet again at the end of February 1840. Still no reply. A long statement was taken from Carron's ex-lodger, John Lloyd (who could well have been the anonymous letter-writer), which revealed that Carron had asked him to leave his house *just before the murder had taken place.* Lloyd also revealed that he had seen Carron just before his sudden departure—in an agitated and distressed state—supposedly because creditors were threatening to put him in prison. Carron did indeed have creditors, but Beresford then took statements from them showing the sums to be paltry and the tales of threats false. 'I have no doubt that if I had been permitted to question Lloyd further information might have been elicited from him,' he complained, when appending some new evidence one of the creditors claimed Lloyd had given him.

Eventually, Pearce wrote to Cartwright again, under cover of a letter from his sister. She received a reply from Cartwright complaining that, after going to much expense in making fruitless enquiries about Carron, he was surprised that he had not received a reply to the three letters he had written to Inspector Pearce. He promised to write again none the less, but never did. A letter from Mrs Carron was then found at her father's house in Lisson Grove, asking that replies be sent to Cartwright via New York post office. Obviously Carron and Cartwright were now hand in glove.

'Inspector Pearce is of the opinion' (said Inspector Pearce in another of his reports) 'that if a person of good judgment and fully acquainted with all the circumstances attending this murder, were to proceed to New York, and to enter with caution upon an inquiry into Carron's mode of life, his means, and his acquaintance with Cartwright, it would lead to evidence sufficient to implicate Carron in the murder—if not to prove him the actual perpetrator.'

There is no evidence that Pearce got his trip to New York, but there is correspondence in the file regarding a Donald McLeod who was given information on the case before he crossed the Atlantic on the *Arcadia* in November 1842; however, I could find no trace of the results of this endeavour. Suspects and alleged sightings of the stolen property continued to surface as late as 1854. In 1841, an English boy from a brig docked at Quebec reported a man, 'very dull and cast down looking and very heavy about the eyes' (and broadly answering Carron's description), approaching him on the quayside and questioning him about the Westwood murder. In 1849 a convict in Bermuda named the lodger, John Lloyd (who in the interval had been transported, had returned, and had dropped out of sight), but Beresford, now a superintendent, thought the informer only wanted to be brought to England—a common ploy.

Despite their failure on the Westwood murder, the police had done good work in a very complex investigation; and Inspector Pearce and Sergeant

Otway began to make frequent appearances in various cases. In February 1840 they chased embezzlers to Calais. In March they prevented a duel on Wimbledon Common between Prince Louis Napoleon Bonaparte and Comte Léon (said to be Napoleon Bonaparte's bastard son), and in May 1840 they were called in on two more murders.

The first of these was another particularly brutal burglary and murder of an old man, a Mr Templeman, this time in Islington in north London. The case had already been botched by the local (N Division) police, who had been handed the murderer, Richard Gould, on a plate by the observant couple with whom he lodged. But although there was evidence Gould had been planning a robbery, they found little which tied him in with this particular one, and failed to consolidate the evidence they already had. Gould was acquitted of the murder, and the police got word that he was on board ship about to leave for Australia. Another bird was about to fly—but maybe they could get him on the robbery charge? Otway set about 'tracing him out'; and while he was gone, Pearce was called in on a case so big that, on hearing of it, Richard Mayne himself hurried to the scene.

4

THE CANDLE FACTOR

WHILE SOME ASPECTS of historic crimes may often appear familiar, others link them clearly to their time. Cut-throat murders, for example, are unusual now, but before the invention of the safety razor they were commonplace; the 'candle factor' is a similar matter.

The whereabouts, condition, type, and value of the candle and/or candle-stick were inevitably important clues in any murder committed after dark during the early Victorian period, as they had been in the Westwood and Grimwood murders. At dusk, candles or oil lamps were lit as an essential aid to indoor movement, and their whereabouts at a murder scene could give valuable clues as to where people had been as opposed to where they said they had been. Intruders often needed them to light their way out, usually dumping them on the doorstep, a point not lost on those wishing to make a crime look like an outside job. Gas lighting had recently been intro-duced, but its use was limited to a few public places. Thus, even in the murder of a wealthy aristocrat, the candle factor inevitably came into play.

Lord William Russell, uncle of the champion of police, Lord John, was an elderly and rather pernickety widower living a well-ordered, comfort-able life in a small but elegant house just behind Park Lane in Mayfair. Though a member of the great Whig family, he had found himself too delicate for the rough and tumble of Parliament and had withdrawn into a life largely concerned with the raising of his seven children and his interest in art—he assisted his brother, the Duke of Bedford, to choose sculptures with which to adorn Woburn Abbey.

The first the police heard about anything interfering with Lord William's hitherto smooth-running existence was at 7.30 a.m. on Wednes-day, 6 May 1840, when PCs Baldwin and Rose of C Division were attracted by the commotion emanating from, and people running towards, the Russell residence at 14 Norfolk Street (now Dunraven Street). One of Lord William's two woman servants opened the door to the constables. The butler, who should have been in control during such a crisis, was sitting in his pantry with his head in his hands, bemoaning his bad luck in having a master so inconsiderate as to get himself murdered. Upstairs, in his curtained four-poster bed, lay 72-year-old Lord William Russell, his throat cut in such a manner, surgeons later opined, as to cause instant death. 'I shall lose my place and my character,' whined the manservant to Inspector John Tedman of D Division and a sergeant who arrived soon after the PCs.

At 5ft. 7½in., Tedman had made the required height with half an inch to spare when he became one of the first new policemen in September 1829. His lack of stature had not prevented his promotion to sergeant the following year and making the rank of inspector by early 1836 — though it probably blocked his entry to the elite land of giants, A Division.

Park Lane was not on his division, but his station house in Marylebone Lane was nearer than C Division's Vine Street, from where Inspector Henry Beresford soon hastened to take his rightful place in charge of the case. He was quickly followed by Superintendent Baker, Commissioner Richard Mayne, surgeons, and the multitude who were to surround the premises almost constantly from that moment on.

Rumour spread that Lord William Russell had committed suicide, and a horrified Queen Victoria sent a message to Sir John. He arrived at the Palace, white-faced and shaken, to give her the truth of the matter. Clearly, this was a case in which there was going to be great pressure on the police. Lord John had recently relinquished the post of Home Secretary to become head of the Colonial Office and already had public sympathy, having recently lost both his wife and father.

That the New Police were at last learning something is shown by the fact that, instead of dashing off hither and thither 'in pursuit', they sent out their route papers while themselves staying put to take stock. In fact, the first thing they did was to inspect the back entrance, which had been found unlocked, to see if there was any evidence of its being forced. What had first alerted the housemaid that there was something wrong was the chaos she found in Sir William's writing room when she came down that morning. Then she had discovered some valuable objects left in a heap near the unlocked front door and more chaos in the dining room — all of which indicated an aborted attempt at burglary. Some valuable objects were known to be missing, but it was not certain which and how many, Superintendent Baker told the commissioner the next day, since the valet, François Courvoisier, was a foreigner and had only been in the job for five weeks. Inspector Beresford searched the servants' personal boxes, and in

Courvoisier's found a chisel, the blade of which he compared with the marks left on the pantry drawers which had been forced to get at the silver spoons. They matched, but (as he was to say in evidence) he thought it better not to challenge the manservant at this stage. The reticent Beresford's heart must have sunk when, at 5 p.m., Inspector Nicholas Pearce of A Division arrived on the scene.

At the inquest, Beresford told the jury that he decided that some marks at the rear entrance were intended to give the appearance of the door being forced from the outside when they had, in fact, been made when it was already open and with some blunt instrument. 'I suggested to Inspector Pearce', he went on, 'that we should search for it . . . I found the poker belonging to the pantry, which was bent and the end or point fitted the latch or socket which had been wrenched off from the door.' Beresford must have been pleased when the subsequent *Times* report of the inquest declared that Inspector Pearce of A Division had nothing to add to what had been said.

By now it had been established that some valuable items, including rings and fob watches with seals, were missing from his Lordship's bedroom. Two others made a mysterious appearance. These were a holder containing a burned-out wax candle and a library book, *The Memoirs of Sir Samuel Romilly*.[1] The valet insisted that he had left Lord William reading this book by the light of the candle, but his housemaid, previous valet, and family all insisted that the victim never read in bed and never had a candle left in his room, for fear of fire. Usually, Lord William would ring for his valet at about 11 p.m. to light him upstairs with a lamp. Once there, a rush light in a shade was left burning — and this was always burned-out by morning. However, on this occasion it was only a third used. Beresford experimented with a similar rush light, and found that it took one and a half hours to burn down by a third. Surgeons had already ascertained that the victim had been dead for several hours when found, so it was quite probable that the rush light had been put out at the time of death.

Several possible suspects, including previous valets and other servants, such as the coachman and the groom, who lived off the premises, 'satisfactorily accounted for themselves'; but Carr, an out-of-work servant who had visited Courvoisier the evening before the murder, was still outstanding. As the inquest ended, the hunt was on for him, although there seems little

[1] A distinguished Whig politician and lawyer, whose anti-slavery and anti-capital punishment stance had been supported by Lord John Russell, but who had committed suicide in 1818 following the death of his wife.

doubt that from the start Courvoisier was the chief suspect. The stumbl-ing-block was that the police had no evidence that he had left the house since the murder — so where was the stolen property? According to Super-intendent Baker's official report, Inspector Tedman, a sergeant, and a P C had been left 'in charge of the premises and property'. But *The Times* knew differently: the officers were there to keep Courvoisier 'under surveillance'.

The 23-year-old Swiss valet was a man of charm and good appearance, and his attentiveness had endeared him to his previous employers. But this had been his first unsupervised post and Sir William had found him wanting, particularly so on the day before the murder, when he had failed to pass on a message to the coachman that the latter should pick up his master from Brooks's Club. He had lied about it afterwards, and also, the housemaid revealed, informed her what he would do if he had half of 'Billy's' money: 'I wouldn't remain long in England.'

Carr was soon found, questioned by Beresford, and released. By Friday, 8 May, only two days after the murder, *The Times* was complaining that the Metropolitan Police seemed without a clue in yet another 'foul and horrible crime'. They were a splendid idea as a preventive force, *The Times* went on, but they were bound to fail at detection due to the semi-military nature of their regulations and all their other duties. The Runners should be recalled. They were experienced, while 'a great portion' of the New Police were even strangers to the Metropolis and for the most part quite ignorant of the various haunts of London thieves, 'and destitute in that sagacity which long experience alone can give of the habits, and oeuvres, and windings, and infinite intrigues of the pernicious "corporation" (for so they may be called) of the thorough-bred villains who infect the metropolis and its environs'.

Those who were now on duty, night and day, in 14 Norfolk Street *were* sagacious enough to notice that Courvoisier grew more agitated when they looked around his pantry. Pearce undertook a more thorough search of the house, bringing in workmen to assist, and two E Division officers who had a reputation for finding things: Constable Collier and a meek-mannered, sharp-eyed sergeant named Frederick Shaw who had been part of the team on the Westwood murder. But it was Pearce himself who discovered, tucked away behind the skirting board in the butler's pantry, a beribboned Waterloo medal and a gold net purse containing gold rings and coins — the property of Sir William. Collier and Shaw winkled out further possessions from under water-pipes, amongst the lead in a sink which the workmen removed from the pantry, and behind a brick in the passage leading to the pantry. The butler denied any knowledge of these items; and the rum thing was that other bulkier property known to be missing, such as the silver spoons, were nowhere to be found.

None the less, Pearce (or, more likely, Mayne) decided they had enough evidence to arrest Courvoisier. He was taken before the magistrates at Bow Street on the following Monday morning—in the charge of Inspector Pearce, who gave all the evidence, and suddenly appeared to the Press to be the one who had done all the finding of pokers and hammers. Beresford was off making further enquiries about Carr, who now appeared to be a more suspicious character than the inspector had at first supposed.

The next day, according to *The Times*, Inspector John Tedman of D Division and Sergeant Smith from C quitted the house at last, to attend Sir William's funeral in the village of Chenies in Hertfordshire. There, 'in deep mourning, with silk hatbands', the two policemen led the cortège from the rectory to the chapel containing the tombs of numerous Russell ancestors. Behind them came the undertaker and the Duke of Bedford's agents 'with silk hatbands and scarves', two mutes on horseback, and six principal tenants of the Duke of Bedford 'in deep mourning with silk hatbands'. The coffin was 'draped in purple cloth richly studded with gilt nails' and carried on a horse-drawn hearse, decorated with velvet and plumes, which was flanked by porters with silk hatbands and staves. Three mourning coaches followed, carrying only close members of the family, since the wish was for the affair to be private. The whole procession was escorted by pages carrying wands, and watched by respectful villagers who lined the route.

On the day after Courvoisier's committal to the Old Bailey for trial, *The Times* published a long letter answering the newspaper's criticism that the New Police lacked detective skills. It agreed that the government had unadvisedly and hastily destroyed a system of detective police which had progressed greatly from the crude and imperfect system instigated by Sir John Fielding until it was almost perfect. What was needed now, suggested the signatory, 'DETECTOR', was to select 20 to 30 Metropolitan officers and add to them the best of the now unemployed Bow Street Runners to form a detective force. This should operate in plain clothes and be paid at the rate now earned by inspectors, plus the other emoluments— presumably the expenses and rewards which the Runners enjoyed. (The principal reasons why many ex-Runners failed to join the police were the low pay and the over-strict discipline.)

But it was over just such emoluments that things began to get sticky for the New Police once the trial (a sensational, ticket-only affair for the gentry) began. The items found on the premises had not been in the original list sent out to pawnbrokers and refiners, and had only been found on the day a reward of £400 was announced. To forestall the obvious accusations, prosecuting counsel, Mr John Adolphus, raised the matter first, and pointed out that the £400 would have to be divided among a great many people, and that the police were unlikely to forfeit a man's life for their paltry share. As for some allegedly bloodstained gloves and handkerchiefs since found in Courvoisier's already-searched box, prosecuting counsel was not going to attribute any weight to these.

During his long and scurrilous opening speech (implying that foreigners are more likely to murder when they rob) Adolphus criticized the police (whom he was representing) for not taking the accused into custody immediately. More strangely, he claimed that the candle had been so far away from the bed that, for the purposes of reading, his Lordship 'might just as well have left it in the cellar'. This despite the fact that Tedman, who gave the principal police evidence about the contents of the bedroom, had already said in evidence that the candle would have thrown light on Lord William's face. He was to repeat this at the trial, claiming that a person in that bed could read from the candle even though he would not be able to reach it. The prosecution's case was mainly circumstantial. Neither bloodstains (the gloves being virtually discounted) nor stolen property had been found on the valet. P C Baldwin, the first police witness, did not help. He made a bad impression by first claiming not to have known about the reward, and then having to admit that the details had been read out at the station house. To aid the jury, 'a very beautiful model of the house of Lord William Russell' was placed on the table, and Pearce brought along a door and door-post with a carpenter and builder as an expert witness. He had experimented on the door and post with a hammer—similar to that found in the pantry—to see whether the marks corresponded. His expert, not surprisingly, thought they did, and that the poker was used to force off the hinge *while the door was open*—he had examined same with a magnifying glass.

Charles Phillips, the brilliant but volatile defence counsel, learned that the Inspector had 'experimented' on *two* doors with a hammer similar to the original one — why had he not brought the other one into court as well? he asked Pearce on the second day of the trial. 'Because I did not think it requisite to do so,' Pearce replied rather pompously. One was enough to illustrate to the jury, he added, when pressed. Why a similar hammer, persisted counsel, why not the real thing? 'Because I was fearful I might thereby alter the state of the hammer,' Pearce replied. No, he had not brought the hammer he used as he didn't think it would be wanted. Pearce suffered quite a punishing cross-examination in the witness box, as had Beresford in his now fairly minor role—the more impressive Tedman being the other chief police witness. The reward kept rearing its ugly head. Pearce claimed he had not heard of it until after finding the missing items.

'Do you expect to get any of this reward if the prisoner is found guilty?' defence counsel enquired.

'Yes.'

'Have you formed any notion of what your share of the reward will be if the prisoner should be convicted?'

'No.'

'If the prisoner is acquitted, you will of course get no reward?'

'None.'

By then, however, it was all up for the defence. At the beginning of this (the second) day, prosecuting counsel had announced that important new evidence had come to light. Phillips, understandably furious that the defence had not been informed of it earlier, blocked an immediate statement to the jury. Small wonder that it was on that day that the accused was noticed by reporters to to have looked really depressed for the first time. This was the evidence which would hang him.

The previous evening Richard Cumming, a solicitor, had arrived at Marlborough Street Police Office carrying a parcel containing the missing spoons. It had been given to him by a French woman, Charlotte Piolaine, the manageress of a Leicester Square hotel. She claimed that the accused (an ex-employee of hers whom she knew only as 'John') had left the parcel in her care 'about six weeks ago on a Sunday evening'. She had not come forward earlier because, despite the fact that the capital was talking of little else, she spoke to few English people and read no English papers. However, her cousin, Joseph Vincent, who was part-owner of the hotel, had seen a mention of the missing silver in a French newspaper. The item had suggested that, since the suspect was Swiss, the London police should look in their foreign quarters, such as Soho, for the loot. Someone there could be looking after it for him. Vincent showed the newspaper to Mme Piolaine, who remembered the parcel, went to a solicitor, and subsequently identified Courvoisier as 'John'.

When, at the end of that second day, Madame Piolaine and another witness to the passing of the parcel were brought forward as witnesses,

Charles Phillips tried vainly to discredit the hotel as a common gaming house. Next day, in his closing address, he gave an impassioned defence of the poor foreigner in a hostile land, complaining again of the lack of time to refute these allegations. He attacked prosecuting counsel for his jingoistic comments and the police for their suspect evidence (all except Tedman, whom he thought gave his evidence most fairly). Baldwin had done his best in the conspiracy to 'earn the wages of blood', and Pearce had tried to extract a confession by asking the valet to dare to look him in the face when he showed him the object he'd found.

'Merciful God! was there an exhibition on earth so likely as to strike him dumb with horror as the proofs of the murder lying before him, and that miscreant challenging him to look him in the face?' He condemned Mr Mayne and Mr Hobler (one of the prosecuting solicitors) for allowing such an interview. 'Such treatment was worthy only of the Inquisition.' One wonders what he would have made of today's police interrogations, now accepted as essential. He also attacked the model of the premises of 14 Norfolk Street as being incomplete — not showing the servants' quarters or other important features; but most of this offensive was an act of desperation — made even more desperate, it was later revealed, because in fact Phillips was already aware that his client was guilty. As he was to admit in a letter to *The Times* nine years later, on hearing of the surprise evidence the Swiss valet had sent for his counsel and had informed him that he was guilty but nevertheless expected to be defended to the utmost.

Courvoisier was found guilty and sentenced to death, but before he left this world he made three more confessions — each one different. The first was on the lines that he had been led from the straight and narrow path by drink and certain circumstances — this in the hope that sympathizers might intervene on his behalf. He claimed that he had been inflamed by reading sensational literature, and by other servants' tales of their more exciting lives with masters who socialized and travelled a great deal. This had led him to begin stealing from his employer who, that fateful night, had caught him staging a burglary. Lord William had dismissed him and threatened to blacken his name. In the heat of the moment, and while a little drunk, he had committed the murder. He also did his best to make the police look foolish by detailing how he had had all the coins, brooches, etc. on his person all the time, and had thus hidden them right under the noses of the police.

After the first confession the commissioners thoroughly investigated the allegations, going through the confession point by point, refuting where possible, and pointing out other discrepancies which did not involve police. But, even in his last confession before death, Courvoisier insisted that he had never been searched before the Friday (Tedman had said he conducted the search on Wednesday, the day of the murder, and it is difficult to believe he would neglect to do this) and that he hid things under the noses of the police. This second allegation may have been true; keeping a person's every move under constant surveillance is virtually impossible, particularly when they are on their home ground. On the other hand, he may have been merely vindictive and/or vain to the last. It is difficult to ascribe rational motives to habitual liars, which, Courvoisier admitted to the Swiss chaplain, he had always been. It is known, moreover, that he even told one lie in the final written confession when he repeated the story that, to avoid getting bloodstained when committing the murder, he had merely rolled up his sleeves. He finally revealed to Mr Evans, one of the under-sheriffs, who looked after him at the last and to whom he had taken a liking, that the reason his clothes had managed to stay so miraculously unstained was that he was naked at the time.

The issue of the gloves was sorted out to some extent by the prosecution solicitors Mr Wing and Mr Hobler, who stated that when the gloves were produced at Bow Street they had seen the accused point out to Mr Flower, his solicitor, a wound or cut on his hand, as if accounting for the stains, and thereby acknowledging the gloves to be his. The problem of the candle was never really explained. Why cook up a story about Lord William reading in bed and leave a candle and book there to prove it? It is possible, of course, that Courvoisier was aware of the fate of the author of the book and was trying to hint that Lord William (who also continued to mourn his wife, although she had died many years earlier) had been inspired to take a similar way out.

In *Two Studies in Crime*, Yseult Bridges puts forward another of the more plausible theories. Courvoisier had lit his way to Lord William's bedroom with a *wax* candle taken from the dining-room, where he had been busy faking the burglary. While committing the murder he had accidentally extinguished the rush light—possibly the spurting blood had done it— lit his way downstairs to wash, then back to his own room. In the morning, suddenly realizing that a *wax* candle in a silver holder might look suspicious in a servant's room, he thrust it and a book into his master's bedroom and left it there. Servants were only allowed tallow candles for personal use, and while two of these were found in the female servant's rooms, no candles whatsoever were found in that of Courvoisier.

5

COUNTDOWN

WERE THEY TO TAKE THE WORD of a man who thought the occupation of a spy an honourable one? exclaimed barrister Charles Phillips to a jury on 27 June 1840. Could any man be safe if such characters existed? Could they believe the man who was stimulated by gain to procure evidence? It was, he continued, the sort of thing we would accuse the French of—but now it was happening here. However, they, as Englishmen, would know that 'the very atmosphere which such a character breathed was tainted'.

For once, it was not the New Police who were under fire but William Ballard and Henry Goddard, former members of the much-vaunted 'old police' or Runners—now turned private detectives at a guinea a day plus expenses. Only a week earlier, this same barrister in his closing speech at the Courvoisier trial, when attacking Tedman and his colleagues over the gloves and the twice-searched trunk, enquired: 'What would a practical policeman of the old school have done—one of those who, after years of experience and drudgery, were dismissed to poverty in the street, to make way for the regiment!' He proceeded to tell them just how such a paragon would have acted—he would have sent the trunk to a place of safety 'where no miscreant speculating on his share of £400, could have tampered with it'. The character of the old police varied, it seemed, at the whim of a barrister who himself had none too good a reputation for honourable behaviour among his own kind.[1]

While the Courvoisier hearings were in progress, Sergeant Charles Otway continued his efforts in the botched case of Richard Gould. The commissioners had learned that Gould, after his acquittal on the charge of murdering Templeman, the old man in Islington, had actually confessed to

[1] Phillips not only learned of his client Courvoisier's guilt during the trial, but was so overwhelmed by the knowledge that he acted extremely unprofessionally by consulting Baron Parke, the judge assisting, as to what he should do. Parke, probably taken by surprise and said to be furious at being thus embarrassed, told him he must continue.

the assistant governor at the prison where he had been held. Now he was at Gravesend, in a ship about to take him to a new life in Sydney. Could he be induced to confess again? Otway traced him, and told him that a £200 reward was about to be offered by Lord Normanby, the Home Secretary, for the name of the murderer of Mr Templeman. According to statements made later by Gould, Otway suggested that, as he had been acquitted of the murder and could not be charged again, he might as well give them the names of the others involved and thereby earn a useful sum with which to start his new life.

At first, Gould resisted but then acquiesced, giving a statement naming names on the promise of the sum of £100. On the strength of this statement, Otway acquired a warrant and arrested him for the robbery of Mr Templeman. Once at Bow Street Gould retracted his statement, saying he had been coerced by Otway. But other evidence had emerged since the original trial, proving, for instance, that shortly before the murder Gould had acquired a 'dark lantern'[2] like the one found at the scene. Eventually, Gould did reach his desired destination — but in a convict ship, transported for life. He sailed on one of the last vessels to take criminals to New South Wales (though shipments to Tasmania and Western Australia continued after this). During the police court hearings and at his trial Gould (perhaps with some justification) did his best to bring Sergeant Otway down with him. Some of the mud stuck, possibly harming Otway's future career.

Now there was a lull. For about a year and a half there were no truly 'sensational cases' to bring embarrassment to the New Police, and it was around this time that Charles Dickens turned, if not a kindly, at least a fairly non-critical eye on the New Police by including in *The Old Curiosity Shop* an imperturbable constable who 'took Kit into custody with decent indifference'. He had already noted approvingly, in his *Sketches by Boz*, that swaggering and ruffianly apprentices were now easily restrained by 'the wholesome dread of the New Police and a perspective view of a damp station house, terminating in a police office and a reprimand'.

During the lull, policemen continued to be killed while performing their duties. In September 1841 PC James Carroll died of injuries sustained while trying to pacify a drunken mob in Spitalfields, and between 1840 and 1842, no fewer than four policemen were accidentally drowned in the Thames. It is, of course, possible that some of them were pushed while carrying out the Met's new duty of policing part of London's docks. In

---

[2] So called because its light could be covered, making it ideal for use in robberies.

October 1841 Joseph Sadler Thomas died, after suffering for the previous two or three years from 'a severe bodily affliction'. Throughout his last ordeal he had been supported by a public subscription, raised in recognition not only of his good police work as deputy chief constable of Manchester but of the humanity and benevolence he had shown while carrying out his duties.

In March 1842, more than ten years after Thomas had successfully led the Italian Boy enquiry, the Metropolitan Police received the compliment of a request for help such as the Bow Street Runners had once answered. It was from a force outside London who needed assistance to solve a murder mystery in which the trail was icy cold.

Around midday on a Tuesday the previous September, a Mrs Robinson, the wife of 'an independent yeoman' with an estate at Eskdaleside near Whitby in North Yorkshire, had been found with her throat cut so that her head was almost severed from her body. The motive, as common as the means in those hard years, was clearly robbery. Thirty-one sovereigns and some silver were missing.

The fact that the crime had been committed during the day, while Mr Robinson was attending a fair at the nearby village of Egton, caused particular sensation and panic, particularly among the Whitby police, who rushed to arrest one suspect after another, only to release them almost as quickly. Eventually, in November 1841, they lighted more firmly on a Mr Hill, a local miller who was in the habit of calling on Mrs Robinson on Tuesdays to deliver meal. He swore that she had been alive and well when he left her at 10 a.m., but a surgeon declared she had been murdered before then. It was thought that someone who knew the house well had done the dastardly deed — and this was true of Mr Hill. In addition, not only had the miller taken a different way home than usual that day, but his statements to the police and Whitby magistrates also appeared inconsistent. He was taken to trial early in 1842, but the grand jury returned no bill[3] and he was discharged.

Mulgrave Castle, the country seat of the Marquis of Normanby (the previous Home Secretary) was only ten miles from the scene of the crime. The marquis, concerned about the continuing fear, suspicion, and ugly rumour about Mr Hill, went to see Rowan and Mayne. They in turn sent for

---

[3] A 'true bill' was a bill of indictment endorsed, after investigation, by a grand jury as containing a case for court. For a jury to 'return no [true] bill' meant that there was not enough evidence for the case to go to trial.

Inspector Pearce who then proceeded in a northerly direction until he reached Whitby — as *The Times* later reported, 'not in his police uniform but as a private person, and that character he continued to assume whilst he was himself acquainted with the whole of the circumstances connected with the murder'.

It was now more than six months since the death of Mrs Robinson, but Pearce quickly decided that Hill was innocent, and plumped instead for the idea of a person from outside the district. There was evidence suggesting that someone had hidden themselves in the Robinson's cowshed and made a hole in the wall so that they could spy on the house. Nearby had been found the remains of a loaf 'made in a different manner from bread in that district'. Pearce also discovered that a woman servant of the Robinsons had, back in 'turf-time' (July), bumped into Thomas Redhead, a previous servant of the Robinsons purportedly in the area to see a friend — whom he did not, after all, call upon. Redhead's mode of dress tallied with that of the stranger who had been seen around the time of the murder.

Since Redhead had claimed to have arrived in Eskdaleside by the Stockton coach, Pearce went off on one of his chases. He traced his suspect back from Stockton-on-Tees to Hetton Colliery, on to Bishop Auckland in Durham, then back south again to Darlington, finally ending up back in Bishop Auckland again, where he discovered that Thomas Redhead had been living in the nearby village of Shildon[4] but had died of the smallpox three months earlier. Pearce persisted with his enquiries, none the less. He found that Redhead had become an excavator on the Shildon railway tunnel but had been absent for several days in July 1841 (when the servant had seen him) and again from 11 – 15 September that year (at the time of the murder). What was more, he was penniless when he left Shildon, but arrived back the day after the murder with sufficient funds to pay off his debts, buy several things, and invest in a grocery business. As *The Times* later pointed out, 'The distance between the places, Shildon and Eskdaleside, is nearly 50 miles, but as a railway traverses a great portion of the way, it was easy for the supposed murderer to get back the next day.' (Part of his journey would have been on the world's first railway passenger line, the Stockton to Darlington, opened in 1825.)

Despite his newly acquired wealth, Redhead's luck was not to hold. His partner, a rogue named Tomlinson, tricked him out of his grocery shop, and a subsequent court action to reclaim it failed — largely due to

---

[4] Also spelled Shildar and Sheldon by the Press at the time.

Redhead's apparent fear of being seen in court and speaking up coherently. From that time he went downhill, speaking to no one and subject to melancholy and fits of crying. It was reported that as he lay dying he attempted to confess something but never managed to utter it. Pearce arrested Tomlinson, believing him to be involved, but soon decided that Redhead alone had been responsible. This news, whether true or not, certainly pleased the Whitby magistrates enormously, and greatly enhanced the reputation of the Metropolitan Police.

The respite from criticism of the New Police came to an end in the following month; as before, the troubles did not come singly. The first was to bring into focus one of the primary problems of the police at the time — lack of good communications — and cause an enquiry into the proper use and effectiveness of the method employed to combat this: the route paper system. The case in question not only brought renewed attacks on the police, but was also one in which a murderer suffered from extraordinarily bad luck.

At 8.45 p.m. on Wednesday, 11 April 1842, P C William Gardner was patrolling Wandsworth High Street when a pawnbroker complained to him that he had been robbed. An irascible coachman by the name of Daniel Good had come into his shop to buy a pair of breeches; after he had gone, a boy assistant claimed that Good had also lifted another pair and slipped them under his greatcoat flaps.

P C Gardner hastened to Putney and the house of Good's master. He was directed to the nearby stables, where he found the coachman. Good vigorously denied the accusation, but agreed to a search of the harness rooms, carriage houses, and stables — that is, until they got to the final block of stables, when Good became anxious and said, 'Let's go to Wandsworth and make it all right.' But the New Police were learning to appreciate on-the-spot thoroughness, and Constable Gardner said, somewhat primly, 'No, I'll not go until I have searched the stable; and made a diligent search.'

Once inside, his attention having been drawn by Good's shifting about of some straw, he found what at first seemed by the light of a lantern to be a plucked goose. While he was taking a closer look, Daniel Good dashed out, closing and locking the stable door behind him. Later, Gardner claimed his response was: 'Now we are done.' But one of the boys reports a more realistic 'Oh my God, we have lost the prisoner!' — still a cardinal sin in police circles today. At first they struggled to open the door, but then went back to have another look at the 'goose' — which turned out to be a human female torso. It took about fifteen minutes after the flight of Good for P C

Gardner to get the door open and raise the alarm. By four o'clock the following morning, all the stations in the 60 square miles covered by the Metropolitan Police had been informed—a not unimpressive achievement, although the news was acted upon in varying ways.

The Inspector in A Division claimed to have immediately notified the men on the beat, while Inspector Tedman, who received the route paper at 3 a.m., thought it sufficient to read it out to the men of the early shift which paraded at 6 a.m. Unfortunately for him, the woman who turned out to be the victim, Jane Sparks, or Jones, or Good, actually lived on his patch, just off Manchester Square. She had not been seen by neighbours for three days—ever since she had gone off to beard Good at his place of work about the new woman in his life—but it was to her lodgings that Good first hurried. He left again, most conspicuously, at 5.15 a.m., piling a bed, a box, and a large bundle into a cab. Two further cabs got him to Spitalfields and his first 'wife', Old Molly Good. A D Division sergeant traced him there, but so drew attention to himself that Good was warned before the sergeant could act.

It was an embarrassing chapter of accidents, and provoked an inquest on the working of the whole route paper procedure. The superintendent should have got the message out before 11.15 p.m.; it should have been more detailed; once received at stations, the news should have been acted upon with more urgency, and so on. Some officers, including little Tedman, were suspended from duty.

The strong reaction was partly due to the Press, who were indulging in another anti-police field day, publishing every detail of a chase in which the suspect appeared always to be a step ahead of the incompetent and unco-ordinated police. Such chains of events, of course, always look much simpler than they really are when viewed from the outside and in retrospect. *The Times* commented three days after the murder:

> The conduct of the Metropolitan Police in the present case, as in those of the unfortunate Eliza Grimwood, Lord William Russell, and others, is marked with a degree of looseness and want of decision which proves that unless a decided change is made in the present system, it is idle to expect that it can be an efficient detective police, and that the most desperate offender may escape with impunity.

Pearce himself received kinder treatment, not only in the report quoted above, which declared him and Inspector Harris of H Division unwearied though unsuccessful in their efforts to catch Good, but also in a potted version of the Eskdaleside murder which the paper ran alongside, and in which it took pains to remind its readers how this case had been solved by the 'vigilance, skill, activity, and most praiseworthy exertions of an officer of the Metropolitan Police'. A man who had acquired much experience in 'matters of this kind, and who, it will be remembered, apprehended the murderer Courvoisier'. Obviously Pearce, too, had made some friends among the penny-a-liners.

One of the gravest mistakes committed by the New Police was their openness with the Press, probably due to a sense of public duty combined with a certain naivety. This over-frankness was to continue, and was criticized by barrister Serjeant Ballantine, writing forty years later:

> The Old Bow Street Runners did not inform the criminals whom they wanted to catch with what their trap was baited, and where it was to be laid, nor did they waste valuable time making reports. They did not let the public know all that they knew themselves, but arrived at a conclusion from their own experience, and worked it out in silence and secrecy.

Referring to a recent case where the police had let it be known that they had no clues and that the murdered man had died without giving any information, Ballantine went on: 'I suspect that old officers [the Runners], if they had opened their mouths at all, would have been guilty of the pious fraud of saying, "that they had obtained a full description of the murderer".' Which is probably the kind of thing Charles Dickens was referring to when he accused them of never losing a public occasion 'of jobbing and trading in mystery and making the most of themselves'.

Of course, many Press revelations about police movements were actually rumours or mere speculation. If proved wrong, the journals were the first to refute it, with an air of innocence that belied their initial responsibility.

Pearce was put onto the Good case to try to pull things together. They suspected that Old Molly Good was still in touch with the suspect, so Pearce posted an experienced sergeant to watch her house continuously. This was Stephen Thornton, who had been on the Westwood murder enquiry and who was feared by pickpockets at the Epsom Races as being even wilier than they were, possibly because Epsom was his birthplace. Later, he was described by Charles Dickens as having a ruddy face, a high, sunburned forehead, and the air of one who has been a sergeant in the army, 'he might have sat to Wilkie[5] for the Soldier in the *Reading of the*

---

[5] The Scottish painter Sir David Wilkie (1785–1841).

Will'. Thornton had, in fact, enlisted in the army for one year but had been out of work on joining the police in 1832.

To flee successfully requires funds, which the police knew Good did not have, but which Mrs Good, who kept a fruit stall at Bishopsgate, might be providing. Watch was also kept on his new amour, the young Lydia Susannah Butcher, who lived at Woolwich. Meanwhile citizens were sighting the suspect all over the place, and watch was kept at docks lest he should try to escape to New York. There were some convincing reports from Kent which suggested Good might be making for the Channel ports, and Pearce hastened down there. But it was to be a member of the public, albeit one who had served in the Metropolitan Police, who finally located Good.

Thomas Rose, a labourer on one of the ever-extending railway systems at Tonbridge in Kent, had not only been a policeman stationed at Wandsworth, but actually knew Daniel Good, and spotted him one day, working on a building site near the line. The coachman, originally accused of stealing a pair of breeches, was arrested, convicted, and hanged for the murder of Jane Sparks, or Jones, or Good—the woman he had consorted with until another, more desirable one came along. Susannah Butcher would settle for nothing less than marriage, and Good until the last blamed the whole thing on her.

Pearce and Thornton had also acquired evidence against the third woman in Good's life, Old Molly Good, and an accomplice. They were arrested for receiving some of the dead woman's clothes, and for being accessories after the fact—much to the derision of the *Morning Advertiser*: 'The secret of the matter appeared to be that police, feeling annoyed at the slovenly manner in which the case has been managed, as well as their own almost culpable negligence in permitting the murderer to escape, were determined to apprehend some person as a sort of *flash in the pan*.' Sensing that public opinion, whipped up by the Press, was against them, the attorney-general offered no further evidence when the case came to trial, on the grounds that the poor woman was only doing her wifely duty—despite there being considerable doubt as to whether she was, legally, Mrs Good.

While Daniel Good was awaiting trial there came the second dastardly crime of 1842. Once again it was in idyllic, rural Islington. This time the chief victim was a policeman, P C Thomas Daly, who was shot dead while chasing a known criminal or 'highwayman', as some of the Press chose to call him. Another policeman and a member of the public were also shot and injured. There was no mystery or chase, the man being captured instantly; but this time there were questions as to why unarmed police were sent after armed robbers — after all, the Bow Street Runners had carried pistols.

An armed attempt on the Queen's life later that month was the final straw. By the middle of June 1842, the Metropolitan Police had permission for their Detective Branch.

CONSIDERING the well-publicized lead-up, the Detective Department came onto the scene almost unheralded. The new branch was small: only eight strong. There were two inspectors and six sergeants — although the commissioners had wanted eight — and Nicholas Pearce was put in overall charge. The other inspector was neither the accident-prone Tedman, the credulous Beresford, nor even the hard-working, high-profile Field; he was Inspector John Haynes from the P or Camberwell Division. Haynes had acquired something of a reputation for catching horse-thieves, of which there were many in those days, and the knowledge he had thus gained had, oddly enough, proved useful in a case of looting from an Indiaman wrecked off Margate in 1840. Calculating how far the thieves, in a horse and cart carrying 2,000 lb. of goods, could have travelled each day towards London, and thus working out at which inns they would be staying, enabled him to retrieve much of the property. This analytical approach was worthy of an ex-chemist such as he.

The six prospective Detective Branch sergeants whose names appeared on the list sent by Mayne to the Home Office on 14 June 1842 were Gerrett, Thornton, Whicher, Goff, Shaw, and Braddick.

Goff and Whicher were only P Cs at the time, so gained a double step up. Twenty-seven-year-old Jonathan Whicher was shortish, at 5 ft. 7½ in., but thickset. This pockmarked, thoughtful ex-labourer from the then rural Camberwell south of the Thames had been in the New Police for less than five years, but had gained a reputation for being observant and for backing his own hunches. Charles Burgess Goff was the constable who not only had been the first policeman on the scene after the Eliza Grimwood murder but had acted efficiently enough to have been seconded to assist Field in the subsequent abortive chase.

As for those who already held the rank of sergeant, there were the wily, thirty-nine-year-old Stephen Thornton and Frederick Shaw, both of whom had seen tough service on the Westwood and Good murders, and Sergeant William Gerrett, who had worked as Pearce's assistant on the Good murder chase. Sergeant Braddick remains something of a mystery; little is

The memorandum appointing the first members of Scotland Yard's official Detective Branch in 1842. The initials are those of Richard Mayne. All correspondence, police orders, and memoranda were handwritten at that time. (Courtesy of the Metropolitan Police)

15 August 1842

Memo:

Two Inspectors and Six Sergeants are to be employed as a Detective Body, as sanctioned by the letter of the Secretary of State of June 20th:- The following Men are appointed to this duty from the dates against their names:-

A.   Inspector Pearce

P.   "   Haynes

A.   Sergeant Smith

E.   "   Thornton } From the 8th Inst.

L.   Constable Whicher

R.   Constable Goff

"   Sergeant Shaw

F.   "   Braddick From the 10th Inst.

R.M.

known about him other than the fact that he was from F Division. All the new detectives were transferred to A Division on appointment, and the fledgling branch was given offices at Scotland Yard.

For taking on their new responsibilities, the two inspectors gained quite a jump in salary—from £116 to £200 per annum—plus the expectation of additional rewards from the extra important cases they would now handle. The sergeants' pay, at £73, was £10 more than that of their uniformed colleagues. These higher rates were offered to members of the branch 'in order to induce those most competent to enter it and continue to exert themselves zealously without looking to advancement to the other police appointments'. In other words, they should be prepared to remain content with the limited promotion prospects within the Detective Branch.

PART II
THE REAL THING

6

FIRST CASES

EVEN WHILE the new Detective Branch was being organized, a further attempt on the young Queen's life was made — on the very day the perpetrator of the previous attempt, John Francis, had been reprieved from the hangman's noose and sentenced to be transported for life instead. Francis had stepped out of the crowd on Constitution Hill to fire a pistol at the recently married Victoria as she passed by in her carriage. Police were chastised for not noticing his intentions, but they did at least arrest Francis promptly.

The same was not true of the second 'attempt' by the simple-minded John Bean. The boy was disabled (the *Illustrated London News* referred to the attacker as 'a hunchbacked miscreant'), and the police reacted by rounding up any similarly disabled young men — much to the journal's derision: 'This week, the run has been against hump-backs; during the twelve hours for which the majesty of British justice was distanced by that crooked piece of malignity . . . the number of little deformed men "detained", to use a mild phrase, was astonishing. Before one station-house, a whole regiment of these unfortunate individuals was paraded.' The New Police did eventually get their man, and it turned out that the gun had not been loaded properly, and not really aimed at the Queen in any case. But Bean was sentenced to 18 months, and the constables who let him escape in the first place were dismissed. Apart from this, there were no exceptionally serious crimes for the new Detective Branch in their inaugural year; but the men managed to keep busy, despite official worries that there might not be enough work to justify their existence.

In the autumn of 1842, Pearce was informed that an elegant young woman named Viscountess Le Grange had been driven in a splendid carriage to the door of an elegant Pall Mall jewellers, where she proceeded to dupe the establishment out of four diamond rings. Pearce had a shrewd idea who the 'Viscountess' might be, and proceeded to 'trace her out' to Dublin. Back at Bow Street he was able to connect her activities with another jewel thief, 'Baron Kane'. The *Illustrated London Life* described them variously as 'foreign swindlers' and 'fashionable thieves', while depicting Pearce as an inspector or superintendent of A Division and referring to Sergeant Thornton, who was also involved in the enquiry, as 'Constable Thornton of the Detective Force'. The launching of the new Department had been so low-profile that the Press had not yet properly distinguished them from the rest of the police force.

The following July, Pearce brought two 'extremely well-dressed young Germans' to Marlborough Street police court,[1] one of whom had been 'figuring about on horseback assuming to be a man of property and fashion' while the other acted as his 'guide and interpreter'. After billing their case a 'Daring Swindle by Foreign Thieves', the *Illustrated London Life* revealed that the police believed them to be members of 'an organized gang of foreign predators who periodically visit this country'. This, of course, was reported when nothing had yet been proved against them.

The one attention-attracting murder during this period, that of Peel's secretary by Daniel McNaughton, required no detective expertise. The culprit was arrested on the spot by a PC and a superintendent. McNaughton had imagined he was killing Peel himself; he was acquitted on the grounds of insanity, and ordered to be detained in an asylum. This verdict was felt to be unsatisfactory, and eminent judges were consulted. Their rulings, which allowed for a 'guilty, but insane' verdict, became known as the McNaughton rules.

Another sensation, a prosecution following a duel which resulted in the death of Colonel Fawcett, brought credit for persistence to the uniformed Inspector Aggs—the man who had failed to solve the murder of barmaid Eliza Davis and had had such difficulty recouping his expenses. He still had money on his mind. After praising Aggs's 'indefatigable exertions' in the Fawcett duel case, the *Illustrated London Life* commented:

> To Inspector Aggs, whose zeal and ability have so much distinguished him during the late prolonged investigation, must be given the exclusive merit and credit of having discovered the name and residences of the seconds. It is likely that the Commissioners of Police will do more than repay him the expenses he must necessarily have incurred in order to procure information. The case, we think, would justify their granting him some gratuity, if not as a reward, yet as a matter of encouragement to others in his situation.

---

[1] They ceased to be called police offices when their police were withdrawn in 1839.

What the commissioners seemed more concerned with at the time was rewarding Pearce for his work in getting his department up and running and giving him some inducement to remain in charge. Towards the end of 1844 they applied to the Home Secretary for permission to raise Pearce's salary from £200 to £250 — which would bring him up to the level of a superintendent's pay. What they had feared had happened. There was a vacancy for a superintendent in F Division, which then covered the Covent Garden and Bow Street areas. Both the Detective Branch inspectors wanted it, and Pearce, particularly, was more than qualified. As Mayne pointed out, 'it would be an injustice to pass him over'.

The Home Office pointed out that Pearce received rewards, in addition to his salary. Pearce and Haynes duly itemized the payments on conviction they had received since the Detective Branch was launched. They totalled around £75 each, which (Mayne explained) did not recompense them for their continuous expenses travelling around the district, some of which, for various reasons, they could not claim back. But an anonymous official at the Home Office did not agree, as an unsigned note on the Home Office file reveals:

> The situation of Detective Inspectors is in many respects preferable to that of a Superintendent. He has not so much active out-of-door service, not so much hard work to undergo: and the peculiar business in which he is employed would be much more interesting to a police officer than the routine business of Superintendents. Besides, he is one of two, instead of being one of a body of officers; and there is more room for the exercise of skill, more opportunity of fame, in his calling and duties, than on those of a superintendent so that upon the whole, the service is in many respects preferable. £250 with the Rewards seems much too great a salary — especially when it is remembered that the Superintendent never receives rewards: his business being entirely unconnected with thief-taking.

Besides (the note went on), if Pearce were granted a rise the superintendents would then start claiming more. 'I do think it would have been better', was the cryptic closing comment, 'if this application had never been sent in by the Commissioners.' The writer was probably the permanent under-secretary, March Phillips. According to Douglas G. Browne,[2] Phillips and Mayne disliked each other. So the request was refused; within a matter of days, the father of Scotland Yard's Detective

[2] *The Rise of Scotland Yard.*

Branch was gone from it, to become Superintendent of F Division, his place being taken by Inspector Joseph Shackell.

It has been claimed that, while the 45-year-old Shackell had applied to join as soon as the department was formed, he had not previously shown any pronounced bent for detective work. This is possible, but the man certainly had some valuable experience. He had joined the Metropolitan Police immediately they were formed in 1829, had seen service in several divisions, and been promoted to inspector within eight months. None the less, in 1834 he left to become gaoler at Bow Street police office. Standing about in the courtroom probably caused the varicose veins from which he later suffered, but the job was not entirely a static one. He became involved in several investigations, including 'the alleged attempt to disfigure Madame Vestris'. Madame Vestris was a celebrated theatrical figure of the time who had been sent what appeared to be a bomb — which Shackell was dispatched to inspect. He had also aided Bow Street Runner Henry Goddard in the daring arrest of the armed and immensely popular Chartist 'torchlight agitator', Reverend Joseph Raynor Stephens, at Ashton-under-Lyme in March 1839. In his capacity as Bow Street gaoler, Shackell became sufficiently well known to be referred to in Press reports by his surname only. But in December 1839, after Bow Street lost its remaining police powers, he rejoined the Metropolitan Police as an inspector. The commissioners obviously felt highly of him to promote him to the fledgling Detective Branch.

Not long after his arrival, the department was set the task of tracing 'extensive robberies of lawns and silks', the proceeds of which were apparently received at a Smithfield pub frequented by butchers. The smooth-faced Sergeant Henry Smith, 'a dab hand at housebreakers',[3] was elected to become one of them — fresh up from the country and looking for work. At the time of the Popay incident there had been complaints about policemen disguising themselves in anything from gentlemen's clothes to sailor jackets or ploughmen's smock frocks. The commissioners had claimed that this practice was vital to the catching of pickpockets, and the Runners certainly had not flinched from such practices: in his memoirs, Goddard proudly recalls that, when Shackell and he were in pursuit of the Chartist leader in 1839, he made himself incognito so that he could mix with 'ruffians of the lowest type'. As for the extraordinary variety of the disguises adopted by the early New Police, Belton Cobb suggests that this

---

[3] Charles Dickens, 'The Detective Police', *Miscellaneous Papers*.

could be accounted for by the fact that the men ordered to wear plain clothes (or 'coloured clothes' as they were termed) put on whatever they possessed — 'usually the dress of their last employment'.[4]

This was the case with Smith. When hearing of the exploit later, Charles Dickens, a dedicated amateur actor, found Smith's casting as a yokel butcher inspired:

> Never, surely, was the faculty of observation better brought to bear upon a purpose, than that which picked out this officer for the part. Nothing in all creation could have suited him better. Even while he spoke, he became a greasy, sleepy, shy, good-natured, chuckle-headed, unsuspicious, and confiding young butcher. His very hair seemed to have suet in it, as he made it smooth upon his head, and his fresh complexion to be lubricated by large quantities of animal food.[5]

In fact Smith, who hailed from West Thurrock in Essex, had been a butcher before he applied to the Metropolitan Police in 1837. Now he posed as a Northamptonshire yokel at sea in the big city, and took lodgings at the suspect pub. At first he was treated with suspicion — and even followed when he went out to attempt a meet with Sergeants Kendall and Shaw. But eventually he was accepted, the *habitués* taking him under their wing and showing him the London sights — including Newgate. When the landlord made a good buy of stolen lawn or silk from the warehouse porters who brought it in, he stood hot suppers or dinners for all, including the yokel butcher-boy. Smith stayed at the pub for ten weeks, gathering information — and always finding fault with any jobs offered him when his new-found friends took him around the markets to get him placed.

He was ten weeks 'never out of the Butchers' dress — except in bed' before the pub was raided and, for appearances, he was arrested along with the others — despite the landlord insisting that he had nothing to do with it and was truly an innocent abroad. Later, Smith bumped into one of the suspects who had slipped the net. He told him that he was going to lie low for a while at the Setting Moon, a 'snug house' or criminals' hideout in the Commercial Road — and invited Smith over. The sergeant went the following day, taking 'a friend' with him, and arrested the man.

When smooth-faced Smith, this time in his high-buttoned police uniform, stepped into the witness box at the second Bow Street hearing of the case, there were groans of horror and dismay from the dock. Five out of the seven arrested were convicted and some of them transported.

---

4 *The First Detectives.*
5 'The Detective Police'.

THE REAL THING

THROUGHOUT SATURDAY the usually quiet and most
respectable suburban hamlet of Hampstead was thrown into a state of
the most painful and intense excitement by the discovery of a murder
and highway robbery in its immediate vicinity, which, for cold-
blooded atrocity and brutality, has not for many years been equalled.

This statement by the *Observer* may have been the usual excitable
journalese, but the circumstances of the murder in question were unusual,
to say the least. Around 7 p.m. on the evening of Friday, 21 February 1845,
on a particularly cold and frosty day, Mr Hilton, a baker, was calling with
his wares on a Mrs Bakewell in Haverstock Terrace, West Hampstead,
when he heard distant cries of 'Murder!' coming from a nearby field. They
sounded female. 'I thought that some man was beating his wife,' he said
later. 'I entered the field to the extent of 20 rods, but then I heard no more
cries.'

When Hilton asked Mrs Bakewell's maid if she had also heard the cries,
she said nothing and closed the door on him. But he was sure enough in his
own mind to pass on the information to PC John Baldock, when he met
him a few minutes later. Baldock took a path across the field but found
nothing. However, the local police profile was high that night, and his
sergeant soon hove into view. Together they searched the field again, and
beside some railings, on the frozen ground in the far western corner of the
field, they found the body of a plump man, about 30 years old, with his
head lying in a pool of blood.

There was nothing in the man's pockets to identify him; only a couple of
keys, a tin snuff-box, and a letter signed, 'Caroline', telling the recipient
she was pregnant. But the victim had obviously been a bit of a swell, with
his brown wrapper of fine cloth with velvet facings and black, velvet-
collared bodycoat. His dark blue, single-breasted Valencia waistcoat, the
Observer was to inform its readers next day in an effort to aid identification,
was decorated with 'a small red flower and sprigs'. 'His boots are
Wellingtons, and his linen, which is of the very finest texture, is marked
with a large capital D in indelible ink.' A black handkerchief, white boot
hose, black kid gloves, and a hat completed the picture.

PC Baldock stayed with the body while his sergeant went off for a
stretcher, but he was not alone for long. Whistling along the path came a
slight and dandified young man with a nonchalant air, who exclaimed,
'Hello policeman, what have you here?' On being told he had someone
whose throat was cut,[6] the young man asked, 'Do you think he is dead?' and

---

[6] In fact this was not the case: the victim had been killed by blows to the head.

promptly got on his knees to take the victim's pulse. Having decided that the man was indeed dead, and that it was 'a nasty job' and 'a serious case for the constable', the young man elected to stay with him until the stretcher arrived. In the mean time he offered the PC some brandy to help keep out the cold, and gave him a shilling, confiding that the victim could just as easily have been himself, as he often used this path, going to and from town carrying money, despite warnings from his parents.

By the time the inquest was held at ten o'clock the following Monday morning, the victim had been identified as James De la Rue, an unmarried, 33-year-old piano teacher, who lived just off Euston Square in St Pancras. But there was no clue as to his killer. The ground had been too hard to register signs of a struggle or the footprints of the murderer, but (PC Baldock told the coroner) there was blood on the top rail of the fence 'where his hands had been'.

'What makes you say "his" hands?' asked the coroner.

It was a bloody print of someone's fingers, Baldock replied, and he had not seen blood on the victim's hands.

The coroner, Thomas Wakley, MP for Finsbury, was an exceptional man. A surgeon who hailed from Devon, he was to become known for the improvements he achieved in coroner's court procedures, but his reforming zeal addressed itself to other areas of public concern as well. He founded and edited *The Lancet*, through which he attacked medical malpractice, and fought a campaign against the adulteration of food and drink which led to laws curbing such practices. He was attacked by his own profession in 1842, after army doctors claimed that the severe flogging (150 lashes) a soldier had received had not been the cause of his death a few hours later; the coroner's jury, under Wakley's direction, found otherwise. Dickens, who spoke publicly in Wakley's favour several times, thought him 'nobly patient and humane'.

Wakley now asked De la Rue's brother, Daniel, whether he had any idea who might have done the deed — but cautioned him first that, if so, he was not to say a name out loud. Coroner's courts often acted wrongly in this respect, he felt. 'When evidence which attaches suspicion to any person is made known he sees it and is consequently put on his guard. . . . They read in the newspapers the very things they want to know and they act accordingly.' This was why the murderers of the Marrs,[7] Mrs Williams and Eliza Grimwood had remained undiscovered, and as for Mr Westwood, it had been positively stated that the perpetrator was actually in

---

[7] The first victims in the Ratcliff Highway murders.

the inquest room to hear what he wanted to know. 'Under such circumstances of course,' he went on, 'the police are deprived of the best means of
detecting the offender. It is not giving the police fair play.'

It must have been pleasant for the police to know that *someone* appreciated their difficulties, and it is also interesting to learn that there was
some awareness at the time of the folly of being too open in murder
enquiries. Mr Wakley again put his question to the brother, after
announcing that if his answer was 'yes', he would clear the court. Daniel
De la Rue, who had last seen his brother the previous Sunday, when James
had asked him to get him a ticket for a forthcoming anti-Corn Law
meeting, admitted: 'I have not the slightest suspicion of anyone.' This
news, one could argue, might also give aid and comfort to the perpetrator.

What Daniel could say was that his brother always carried a watch with a
gold guard — made by Grafton of Fleet Street.

'Don't state that,' said the coroner. 'You must not state anything that
may lead to a suspicion of parties.'

It was also divulged that the victim was quite well off (he had previously
owned the house he lodged in but had sold it when his mother and sister
died) and often carried quite large sums of money.

After hearing the surgeon, the baker, and the victim's landlord (also a
baker), the coroner had the court cleared, as *The Times* records, 'of all
strangers, not excepting reporters, remarking that he wished to have some
consultation with the officers of the detective force.' Their meeting lasted
an hour and a half, and when it was done Mr Wakley declared the inquest
adjourned *sine die*. Its reconvening would depend, he announced, 'upon
the information obtained by the police, and upon the success of the
detective force'.

The following evening William Watson, yet another baker, this time
from Turnham Green, informed a local sergeant named Scotney that on
the previous Saturday he had been to see his parents in Portland Town
(now the St John's Wood area) and, while there, had been asked in by their
lodgers, Mr and Mrs Hocker. They had appeared to have come into some
money, and he had been offered rum by their son. Thomas Hocker had
declared himself uninterested in talking about the terrible murder up in
Hampstead, as it was depressing, so he sang a song instead. His father,
however, had seemed a little worried that Thomas had been up to something because the wrist of his shirt was torn; Thomas, however, had
claimed to have done it while romping with some girls. William Watson
hold Sergeant Scotney that he had just heard that the victim was James De

la Rue — and he knew that De la Rue had been a friend of Thomas Hocker.

Scotney went hotfoot to Hammersmith police station, where he informed Inspector Morgan of the news, only to be told he must go to London to pass it on to Inspector Shackell or Haynes of the detective force, who had been handling the case since Saturday evening. Couldn't he go and arrest Thomas Hocker himself? Scotney asked. 'You must go where I tell you,' replied the inspector, brushing aside Scotney's complaints about there being no encouragement to get information if one then had to hand it over. Inspector Morgan had only recently had his fingers burned in this respect, when he had omitted to tell the detective force about a robbery of some plate from the Duke of Richmond. The disgruntled Scotney hastened to Scotland Yard, but could find neither Shackell nor Haynes so, as instructed, told the inspector on duty at the nearby Gardner's Lane police station — now A Division headquarters. His name was Partridge, and after informing his superintendent, he hailed a cab to take Scotney, another sergeant, and himself to Portland Town, where Scotney arrested young Thomas Hocker.

Thomas Hocker lodged a short way from his parents, sharing a room and a bed with his brother James. While Scotney was searching the premises, James said, 'Tom, tell the policemen all you know about it — for he can see you are telling him a lie.' Upon which Thomas produced a watch from under his pillow, admitting that it was De la Rue's but claiming that his friend had given it to him the previous Friday morning — to pawn. He had done so with several other articles over the past few months, Hocker claimed, and produced the tickets.

Later that morning Thomas Hocker appeared before Mr Rawlinson, the magistrate at Marylebone Lane police court, charged with the murder of James De la Rue. After hearing evidence of arrest, and of letters, clothes, and sovereigns found at Hocker's parents' home nearby, Partridge asked for a remand.

'I should like to say a few words, your worship,' interjected Inspector Shackell.

'Have you any evidence to offer?'

'Yes, sir, I have some very important evidence.'

'Let him be sworn.'

Shackell, obviously anxious to establish the participation of the detective department in this important case, told the magistrate that he could prove that the watch produced by Hocker was indeed De la Rue's because it answered the description on a jeweller's receipt he had found on the victim's premises—among obscene prints, letters, and bills. That watch was seen on De la Rue by his landlord's daughter, Shackell declared, at 2 p.m. on Friday. This rather knocked on the head Hocker's claim that he had been given it on Friday morning when he had last seen De la Rue.

Hocker was remanded until the following Tuesday, and Haynes, Partridge, and the department's new inspector, Shackell, got to work. They hurried back to Thomas Hocker's pathetic lodgings, where they found letters, papers—obscene prints—and, tucked away in a cupboard, a bloodstained shirt-wristband. They went on to the parents' lodgings, where Mr and Mrs Hocker handed over a shirt with a wristband missing, muddied and bloodstained stockings, and a mackintosh cape in similar condition. When asked when his son had last worn the cape, Mr Hocker admitted it was when he had gone out that fateful Friday evening. Had he taken a cane? the detectives asked. Yes, said Mr Hocker, a black ebony one. It was found and proved to have a split end. Had Thomas said where he had got the money he had when he came back? Yes, replied the father. He said he had borrowed from a friend, a Mrs Edwards, but he feared that not to be true. 'I have got a sovereign of it and if it is not true, I will give it up.'

The conduct of the father and mother had been fair and straightforward during the whole transaction, Shackell was latter to inform the coroner. Haynes took himself off to see Thomas Hocker in the New Prison (now Pentonville) and made him strip to the buff. In the process he found that all Hocker's clothes, including his drawers, were spotted with blood. In addition, there were two buttons missing from his jacket—of the type found near the body and on Hocker's mantelpiece.

The following morning, the inquest was resumed before a displeased coroner. He was angry that the accused was not present when evidence was to be heard which could militate against him. The commissioners, he said, when they formed the Metropolitan Police, had apparently not deemed the coroners' courts of sufficient importance to give instructions about bringing prisoners before them. Then he put Shackell and Partridge on the spot by asking just what instructions they had had about production of prisoners to coroners' courts. None, they had to admit.

The brother, James Hocker, was very much present, because the coroner had issued a warrant for him on the suspicion that he, too, had been involved, following his curious statement on Thomas's arrest. Mr Wakley heard evidence on that. Then, after a lengthy harangue about Thomas Hocker's rights being violated by his not being present, petty jealousies of magistrates, and attitudes towards coroner's courts which he was no longer prepared to tolerate, Mr Wakley continued the hearing in camera, with the police and witnesses, before adjourning the inquest until Saturday morning.

The trouble between the coroner and the police began in earnest on the following Saturday morning, when Thomas Hocker was still not produced — despite visits by Wakley to the Home Secretary which culminated in the latter granting permission for his production, and despite the coroner writing a letter to the prison governor making this clear. (Delivery of the letter had been put in the hands of the Hampstead police, but the prison governor had insisted that he still needed the magistrates' permission. The police had obtained this and returned with it to the prison — to be turned away again, because the permission was only verbal.) This was all the fault of the police in the first place, the coroner fumed, for not letting him know of the capture of Thomas Hocker earlier than nine o'clock on the morning following the arrest. Had the police informed him earlier, he could have reconvened his court that very day; it would probably have reached a verdict of murder against Thomas Hocker, and he could have gone straight to trial without ever going near police courts — there was a precedent for this. He was right in that he could commit directly to trial (although this is no longer the case); but clearly the police were caught in the battle for power between the coroners and the magistrates of Westminster.

The hapless Hampstead inspector insisted he had sent the message to the coroner at 3 a.m. on the morning of the capture, but, when pressed, could not say by which constable. The hearing was by now in camera again, but the Press were able to report none the less that the man who had given the original information to Sergeant Scotney had told the coroner of the delay before the arrest caused by Scotney's having to go to the Yard to fetch a detective. The aggrieved Scotney was called upon to confirm this, and did so in detail. Mr Wakley evinced appropriate disgust and, after adjourning until the following Monday, called Superintendent May and Inspectors Grey, Haynes, Shackell, and Furlong into a private room. The following Monday, Mr Wakley's inquest was graced with the presence of both suspects, Thomas and James Hocker. The coroner heard all the evidence previously given to the magistrates and that acquired since. Among the new witnesses was Mrs Edwards, of Great Titchfield Street in north Soho — the woman who, Hocker had told his parents, had lent him the money. She emphatically denied this, and told the inquest jury that the accused had been paying court to Sarah Jane Philps, a young woman who lived with her, and who had been most upset by all that had recently happened. 'Is it necessary to call the young woman?' Mr Wakley enquired. The police thought it was, but Mrs Edwards interposed that she hoped the coroner would not let Sarah Jane catch sight of Hocker. Consequently, when she came in, as the *Morning Chronicle* later reported, 'some persons present stood up to interpose themselves between her and the prisoner'. Sarah Jane recounted how Hocker, later on that Friday night, had brought the booty to show her: both the watch and a ring, which he had previously told her he owned but did not wear as he did not care for jewellery. The ring had been to big for him, and there was blood on his shirt front, the result he told her, of cutting his nose while indulging in some horseplay.

During Inspector Haynes's evidence, the coroner was astonished to hear that the stained jacket now shown in evidence had actually been worn by Thomas Hocker when he appeared before the magistrates after his arrest. 'And was it not examined?' he asked. 'It appears not,' admitted Haynes, adding, 'but he had a coat, such as he has now, over it.'

After discharging the brother, James Hocker, from custody, Mr Wakley also got his desired verdict from the coroner's jury: 'wilful murder against Thomas Henry Hocker', and duly bound the witnesses over to appear at the Old Bailey. The hearing at the police court on the following day proved something of an anti-climax, all the evidence now having been heard and a decision on it having been passed. 'You must tell the whole story as if you had never heard it before,' the magistrate, Mr Rawlinson, insisted to Sarah Jane, who she said had nothing to add to what she had said yesterday.

The late arrival and early departure of Detective Inspectors Shackell and Haynes, who were required on another case[8] at the Old Bailey, must also have deprived the proceedings of some of their drama. Mr Rawlinson, possibly piqued at being upstaged, decided not to commit to trial as had been expected, but to adjourn the case for a further week. This delay did retrieve some of his status, for behind the scenes in the same building, further revelations were forthcoming.

P C James Euston, detailed to keep Hocker company in his court cell, reported that the accused had complained about one of the witnesses, a barman who had served him at the Swiss Cottage pub that Friday night and had commented, 'You are a gentleman' because of the size of his tip, but who now claimed he could not identify him. He also mentioned 'that

---

[8] A burglary, after which some of the stolen silks and linens were bought by the landlady of a pub in Drury Lane—possibly connected with the 'butcher's tale', although the landlady appears not to have been charged with receiving.

Baldock, the policeman', and told PC Euston that it was *he* who had happened along when the PC was standing with the body and that *he* had offered the policeman some brandy, which was refused, and a shilling which the officer finally accepted. This put Baldock on the spot, for neither court had heard anything about the man who had stayed with him and the body that night. Consequently, Baldock was the first witness called at the resumed police court hearing the following Tuesday. He admitted all that Hocker claimed, including the fact that he had taken a shilling under pressure; but he said that now he did not think he could identify his body-watching companion, as the man had been muffled against the cold — a stance Baldock maintained throughout, probably in self-defence. He had said nothing about the man because he did not think the matter was important, he told Mr Rawlinson. The magistrate accused him of withholding the evidence because of the shilling. It was his duty to give all the facts — not to judge what was important, he added tartly.

At the end of the reading of all the committal statements, Inspector Haynes stepped forward to announce the arrival of yet another witness who had important evidence to give. The latecomer turned out to be a Mr Henry Nash, who claimed also to have heard the cries of the victim that night. He had stood for ten minutes trying to ascertain *from* where they came from, he told the court, when, running up and bumping into him 'all of a bustle', had come Thomas Henry Hocker.

'It was thought not a little remarkable', commented the *Morning Chronicle*, 'that the witness Nash should have waited to the very last moment before he came forward with evidence of so much importance.' That newspaper had already printed screeds of information on the defendant's life which, it insisted, was gleaned from unimpeachable sources, and had been dropping heavy hints as to what the case was really all about. In the previous two years, it was claimed, Hocker had led 'an idle and dissolute life, not untainted by crime, his principal occupation having been the deluding of females and the meeting of the deceased De la Rue in the field for, it is believed, the worst of purposes'. Hocker had received nearly £150 from De la Rue, 'the whole of which he had squandered in vice and debauchery', but had realized that his victim was not going to pay him any more. In other words, what had been taking place was homosexual prostitution and blackmail.

The *Morning Chronicle* also elaborated on Sarah Jane's evidence, saying how unusually cheerful she had found Hocker that Friday evening and full of insistence that his mind was more at ease than it had been for a long time. Having done away with his fellow-debauchee, the paper was hinting, Hocker may well have felt cleansed.

The source of the paper's information might be deduced from one particular paragraph: 'In the discovery of the leading facts, which will be brought forward at the trial of the prisoner, the greatest credit is due to Mr Shackell, the intelligent and enterprising officer of the detective police.' Also, doubtless, someone who had many Press contacts from his days as the Bow Street gaoler.

So Thomas Hocker was at last sent to the Old Bailey, fully committed, as Mr Rawlinson acknowledged, 'by myself as well as by the Coroner's warrant'. But the trial itself, having in effect already taken place so many times elsewhere (particularly in the newspapers), lasted only one day—from ten in the morning to seven in the evening. No women were allowed in the courtroom, due (the *Morning Chronicle* explained) 'to the peculiar circumstances of the case'. There was, however, a dense crowd of influential males listening as Thomas Henry Hocker was found guilty and sentenced to death.

7

INTERNAL STRIFE

WHILE THOMAS HENRY HOCKER was still awaiting trial, P C John James Allen, of the E or Holborn Division, was on duty at the door of St Giles's old watch-house, now the police station house, at about eleven o'clock one evening when a man dashed out of a house further along the street and ran past him. Running men always give vigilant policemen pause—but they also call for instant decision-making. To pursue or not? P C Allen had seen the man hanging around the area eyeing the prostitutes, and, should it prove that anything untoward had happened, he could doubtless find him again. Besides, the rookeries were a rough area—as the *Morning Chronicle* had it, 'thickly inhabited by persons of the poorest, lowest, most abandoned, profligate and squalid description'. P C Allen decided not to pursue.

Six minutes later a Mrs Palmer, the servant from the house in question (which rented out threepenny rooms to prostitutes), also came running up the street. Panting, she told the officer that a woman in there had been 'stuck'. On investigation, Allen found a plump, middle-aged woman lying on her side by the fireplace in one of the rooms. There was an abundance of blood from the sixteen stab wounds she had received, and (while he was not to know the number at the time) he could not miss the large, black-handled carving knife buried in the back of her neck. 'The woman made a slight move when I drew the knife out,' he was to report later, 'but died immediately.' 'The woman' was a prostitute or, as the *Morning Chronicle* put it, 'an abandoned character', named Mary Ann Brothers, or Tape, and her murder, they assured their readers, was 'one of the most ferocious and deliberate' for many years. Definitely in the sensational cases category.

At half past six on the following morning, over on D Division, Inspector Tedman received information that the victim had cohabited with a man called Meadows who lived in South Molton Street, Mayfair. Tedman, not about to be found wanting this time, hurried there, only to find that the man had gone to his work as a blacksmith in nearby Davies Street. Tedman tracked him down there, and soon established that not only had Meadows been missing from work the previous afternoon but he had stayed out until after eleven o'clock the previous evening. What was more, he had blood-stains on his clothes, his right hand, and his handkerchief—all of which he claimed were from a violent nose-bleed. Tedman immediately arrested him for the murder, although he should perhaps have known by then that he couldn't win—particularly as it was April Fools Day. PC Allen, Mrs Palmer (the servant who had actually caught the murderer in the act), another prostitute witness, and a girl at the shop where the knife was bought, all insisted that Meadows was not the man, and that was that.

In fact, although no one knew his name, many knew the murderer's face quite well. He had advertised himself and his intentions to what seemed a ludicrous extent—asking several prostitutes the whereabouts of Ann Brothers, complaining to them that she had given him 'a loathsome disease', and wondering whether she would recognize him; then coming back later in different clothes and asking the same question again. Meanwhile, he had prevailed upon another prostitute to examine his person to see whether he was indeed infected, but she had found herself unable to come to a definite diagnosis.

The *Morning Chronicle* was soon spreading doom and gloom. The murder had been committed late on Monday night; it was now Wednesday morning and as they had gone to Press, the police had, they knew, 'no sanguine hopes of immediate capture'. By the following morning they were proclaiming: 'Notwithstanding the indefatigable exertions of the police, up to eight o'clock past evening no clue had been obtained' and 'It is much feared, as in the cases of Eliza Grimwood and Eliza Davis . . .'. Murders of prostitutes are particularly difficult to solve, due to the number and anonymity of customers. But in this instance the suspect had almost put out flags, so the newspaper's instant pessimism was somewhat premature. Witnesses, including the cutler who had sold him the weapon, were practically queuing up, and it was only a matter of time. By 5.30 p.m. on the Friday, 4 April, Superintendent Pearce (now of the F Division) had him.

With a strong suspicion (the *Morning Chronicle* told its readers) that the murderer had secreted himself at no great distance from the vicinity where the crime had been committed supported by 'some peculiar facts which had privately come to his knowledge', Superintendent Pearce had proceeded to 10 Belton Street, where he had apprehended the man who was later positively identified. In truth, it was at the home of the suspect's aunt, at 4 Stonecutters Alley (just by where Holborn underground railway station now stands) that Joseph Connor was arrested.

Our old friend Mr Partridge, the professor of anatomy at King's College, informed the Bow Street magistrates that Connor had recently been attending the hospital as an outpatient suffering from 'a loathsome disease'. It was, however, a disease which had *not* been given him by the unfortunate Mary Ann Brothers, for the surgeon who examined her had found no trace of such loathsomeness. The motive which eventually emerged was Connor's fury at having been infected with venereal disease by Brothers (as he thought), which meant he would no longer be able to marry his young cousin as had been planned.

Newspaper descriptions of Connor indicate a striking ugliness. The *Morning Chronicle* revealed that he looked two or three years older than his 19 years, was a man of middle height and appeared strong and hardy. But, they told their readers,

> The expression on his countenance is the reverse of pleasing. There is a settled sullenness and fixedness of purpose in his general aspect, much too marked for anyone to fail being struck with it. His features are remarkably large and striking. His eyes are deeply embedded in his face, and his nose and mouth are of unusually large dimensions. He has a narrow retiring forehead, a long face, and flat cheeks. His head is remarkably thin towards the back part, and is surmounted by an ample crop of long dark brown hair, which looks as if never disturbed by comb or brush. The conformation of the head altogether would form a fine study for phrenologists. The existence of the animal propensities is strongly indicated.

He looked stupid but proved shrewd in the questions he put to witnesses, they went on, and they added self-possession, physical stamina, and nerves of steel to the catalogue of his suspect qualities.

The Detective Branch had been involved in the search for Connor, but it was somewhat droll that the murder itself had taken place almost on Superintendent Pearce's ground (the F and E Divisions shared the St Giles area), and his accidental but successful involvement must have given the commissioners some satisfaction.

Yet again the police were caught in the angry cross-fire between Mr Wakley, the coroner, and the police court — this time, Bow Street. Events took exactly the same pattern: inquest adjourned, awaiting further information; suspect then caught; and subsequent appearance of the accused before the magistrates. On this occasion, however, the coroner was informed of the arrest (no thanks to the police, he made clear) in time to recall his jurors, who then sat waiting with him as the witnesses trickled over slowly from the Bow Street hearing. The accused did not appear at all. This malpractice only occurred in the county of Middlesex, declared the furious Wakley; the Home Secretary, commissioners, magistrates, and Pearce were all involved, but it was the police who were largely obstructing him. They ought to remember that the public, who were being insulted here, paid their wages. The next time the commissioners asked Parliament for money, he would oppose any such request. 'Hear, hear', murmured members of his jury.

Connor came up for trial on the same day as Hocker, but his case was postponed for a month, a delay which caused Pearce problems. As four of his most important witnesses were 'persons of low character', he told the commissioner, 'obtaining a livelihood by prostitution, and having no settled place of abode, we consider them very likely persons to be tampered with, and likely to be got out of the way previous to the trial'. He suggested that, in order to keep them within reach, they should be paid an allowance of a shilling a day—via the workhouse governor. The authorities were understandably nervous about this idea and urged caution, but the plan actually worked—although a sour note sounded during the trial, when the evidence of a new witness was questioned as being merely a compilation of that of others. There were suggestions that Pearce had helped him concoct it, and the judge found it sufficiently dubious to warn the jury against taking it into consideration. It does sound possible that Pearce may have been hedging his bets in case some of his women of low character failed to show up.

But, of course, all evidence—civilian and police—was more suspect while the rewards system was in operation, particularly during the hungry 1840s. It is interesting that the commissioners, when discussing the proposed increase in Pearce's salary to keep him in the Detective Branch, claimed that if rewards to police were abolished 'a beneficial stimulus would be lost'. Without 'such encouragements', they told the Home Secretary, they could not hope that 'the same exertion of extraordinary talent and activity would be continued in pursuit and detection of criminals'.

Again, when the time for the trial arrived it was only a day's work to find the accused guilty and sentence him to death.

Although the commissioners had lost the battle to keep Pearce in the Detective Branch, they were not prepared to lose the benefit of his experience and talent in this sphere. Local knowledge is vital in solving crimes, as is local co-operation, and there had already been some trouble between detectives and senior divisional uniformed officers, the latter complaining of being treated with lack of proper respect. The commissioners put Pearce in charge of a new scheme which helped address both these problems. He was to head a mobile squad against burglars and felons. It would be trained, when possible, by the detective sergeants, and the men recruited by the selection of two promising constables from each division.

WHERE WAS PC 313K Clark? He had been seen, briefly, during the early part of the night shift, but there had been no sign of him since. When the time came for him to report back to Dagenham police station before going off duty at 6 a.m., he failed to appear.

Dagenham village, like several other places on the outskirts of London, had not long been under the umbrella of the Metropolitan Police in June 1846. Some of the populace were none too pleased to see the Peelers. They would much rather have been left alone to carry on with their nefarious activities. These included smuggling from boats in the busy Thames, over the nearby lonely marshes which were only negotiable by locals who knew the tortuous routes. One of the few other ways to earn an often scant living in those parts was by mixed farming or the keeping of smallholdings, trundling the produce into London on a horse and cart, or even on foot. Reactions to the interfering newcomers had not been passive. Assaults and threats were the order of the day, and it was rumoured that some policemen found it politic to follow the maxim, 'if you can't beat them, join them'. Consequently, Dagenham police station had become something of a transit camp, with the most recently threatened or most dubious officers being moved out or on to other beats and officers drafted in from central London to take their place. One such replacement was 20-year-old PC George Clark who, six weeks earlier, had been happily serving at Stepney in the East End.

On arrival at his new station, Clark had been allotted a night beat later described as 'extremely lonely in parts'; it had previously been patrolled by the reputedly vigilant PC Abia Butfoy, who had received a threat he could not ignore. Some constables on certain beats were now allowed to carry cutlasses as well as truncheons—to defend themselves against criminals who might well carry pistols and carbines—and PC Clark's new beat qualified as one of these.

Of course, policemen were still being attacked in highly populated places, the most recent murder being of a Deptford constable who had asked a few drunken people to move along and been beaten to death for his pains. But being quite alone is still more frightening. Who would hear a rattle[1] across the solitary field and marshes? Fortunately, George Clark was a religious young man. Possibly irritatingly so, for he would hand out tracts to his fellow officers and to people he met on his beat, and was unlikely to turn a blind eye to any wrongdoing. But his faith may also have given him courage as he stepped out along the silent, unfrequented stretches of road bounded by duckweed-filled ditches.

When Clark failed to report back to his station on the morning of Tuesday, 30 June 1846, his inspector and superintendent, Richardson and Macquard, mounted a search, and sent a messenger to his widowed mother in Bedfordshire asking whether she knew of his possible whereabouts. His four night duty colleagues claimed not to have seen Clark since they had been marched out towards their beats at nine o'clock the previous evening by Sergeant William Parsons. Parsons, a stocky, sandy-haired Norfolkman with a great many freckles, reported having left Clark at The Four Wants, a crossroads marking the start of his beat, and having met him again at the first of his official fixed points at one o'clock. Shortly after this, Clark had failed to join P C Kempton, who was on an adjacent beat, for their usual meet. Neither did he show up at his next official meeting with his sergeant at three o'clock, Parsons reported.

Lanes were trudged, ditches clambered into, cornfields scanned, and ponds dragged until last light, at around 9 p.m. At dawn the search began again. P C Kempton thought it was all a bit of a waste of time, as he told farmer Ralph Page. Clark's body was probably in one of the cornfields, and they wouldn't be able to find it until harvest time. It was an opinion voiced to Page again that afternoon by three policemen sitting on a gate, taking a break from their warm exertions; but farmer Page disabused them of this notion. A man's body in a cornfield would be easily traced. 'For a dog running into standing corn would leave a track', he told them. At that moment, he was to swear later, Sergeant Parsons joined the perspiring group to report that they had thoroughly searched all the cornfields and found nothing.

On Friday evening, four days after Clark had gone missing, they were still no further forward. P Cs Kempton and Butfoy were dragging yet another pond, this time in Ralph Page's farmyard, when Mrs Page came

---

[1] Clark carried a rattle, but they were at the time being replaced by whistles—only to reappear later before being finally phased out in 1886.

out and told them there was a further pond they might want to look at — the children would show them where. The boys led the two top-hatted, high-buttoned Peelers through a potato field and on into a cornfield, where they instantly noticed a strong and unpleasant smell. Then Kempton found a much damaged police truncheon and, a few yards further on, one of the boys came across a bloodstained cutlass stuck into the hedge bank. It may have been his screams that his mother heard back at the farm for, as he showed Kempton and Butfoy where he had found the cutlass, the boy turned to see the decomposing body of the missing constable. It was not a pretty sight. One of the young policemen, called over from an adjacent field by the cry, 'Here he lies', fainted on the spot when he got there. P C George Clark lay on his back with his legs crossed and his right hand clutching a handful of corn. His face was very bruised and there was a large opening in the top of his skull, with his scalp lying alongside. There were deep cuts to the back and front of his neck and the trodden down corn around his body was saturated with his blood and pieces of his bone.

The next morning, Saturday, 4 July, the details of the finding of Clark's body were laid before the local magistrates — who, it should be said, were themselves culpable, inasmuch that they had not supported the New Police and had been imposing only light sentences on those miscreants brought before them — probably through pique at being usurped, and possibly also through fear and corruption. Now, however, they were suitably aghast, directing the officers to 'use every vigilance in their power' to capture the murderers. But it was not to be left to the local police. 'On the receipt of the intelligence of the outrage at Scotland Yard', said *The Times*, 'two of the most active officers of the Detective Police were sent down to Dagenham.'

In those days before refrigerated mortuaries, they lost no time in opening the inquest, particularly during the summer months. The one on Clark opened the same afternoon at the Cross Keys public house, opposite the church in the heart of the village. Both buildings still stand today, an odd quaint island in an ugly ocean of ribbon development. A surgeon gave the more grisly details of the constable's wounds, and Abia Butfoy related the incident which had led him to be moved to another beat from the one which the unfortunate Clark inherited. A couple of months earlier he had stopped a marine store dealer named Moses Walker and asked him what was in the bag on his shoulder. The man had told him to mind his own business, and a scuffle ensued; Moses had given way and emptied his bag, but, on leaving, had muttered curses and threats that he would revenge himself on Butfoy.

When the detectives, led by Shackell, arrived, they found that another mistaken-identity theory was going the rounds. Perhaps the victim was meant to have been Sergeant Parsons, who had 'rendered himself obnoxious' to some of the more notorious characters of the neighbourhood by arresting one of them — Amos Walker, brother of Moses — for having stolen hemlock in his possession. The plaintiff in that case had not turned up at court, but Parsons had persisted with the charge regarding some other property which was identifiable, and the magistrates had been obliged to convict. But they had imposed only a small fine, advising Walker to be more careful in the future. Robbery was clearly not a motive, since Clark's money and watch (and rattle) were still in his pockets. What *was* missing was Clark's hat. Inspectors Shackell and Richardson sent men out to find it — and to see if they could spot anyone who looked as though they had been in a fight. The search for the hat was hindered somewhat by the numbers of curious people, from Romford, Barking, and the villages in between, now converging on Dagenham and the scene of the crime. It was a miracle that the hat survived, to be found and handed in by a farm labourer on the evening following the opening of the inquest. It had, in fact, been only twelve to fourteen yards from the spot where the body had been found.

When the inquest was reconvened ten days later, there had been no arrest. The reason, thundered *The Times*, was because no reward had yet been offered. The lull between the murder and the finding of the body had meant the culprits, who were probably members of one of the gangs in the neighbourhood, had had time to wash the blood from their clothes, but the chance of a reward would doubtless induce one of them to betray his companions. The inquest, however, did provide some startling new evidence. Just as it opened, the coroner asked the jury if they would mind waiting for half an hour while he took two of them to see a woman who, he had been informed, had vital evidence but had not been called. If there was any truth in the rumour, she would be brought back with them.

The woman turned out to be Ralph Page's wife, Elizabeth, and she was duly invited aboard the chaise which conveyed the coroner and jurors back to the Cross Keys. But before she had a chance to speak at the inquest, Amos Walker stood up to protest that he and his brother were innocent of any murder. It was true they had quarrelled with Parsons and Butfoy, but they were innocent of the other allegation, and wanted to stay in order to listen to the evidence in case it maligned them further. Mrs Page's sensational evidence was worth staying for. She told the jury how, that night, she had loaned the officers a coat to cover the body—for decency's sake. Three of them returned the coat at around midnight and stayed to supper. As they ate, Kempton told Mrs Page that Sergeant Parsons had *not* been on duty for most of the night on which Clark had gone missing. He had been feeling unwell, so had asked Kempton to take his horse and finish his duty for him—which the PC had done. PC Jonas Stevens, one of the officers who had been at supper at the Pages, was then called, but he insisted that he had not heard Kempton say he had done Parson's duty. He thought he probably would have heard—if it had been said. Mrs Page pointed out that *this* was the young constable who had fainted at the sight of Clark's body, and who had been so bad at her house that she had constantly urged Kempton to take him home. In other words, he was in no fit state to notice anything. Kempton denied ever having said anything of the sort, Parsons denied having been absent on the night of the murder, and his other PCs swore to having seen him during the night.

Other questions appeared to be preoccupying the coroner. Why had Clark's box, in which he kept his belongings, been broken open? Why had Clark's mother had difficulty in gaining access to it? And what were Clark's relations with his colleagues? It had been broken open by Clark himself, said his Dagenham room-mate, the fainting PC Jonas Stevens, when he had lost his keys back in Stepney. Despite it having no lock, Stevens admitted that both he and Clark kept their money in the box. Clark had been quite careful with his money and there were rumours that some of the men had been in debt to him, but Stevens denied any knowledge of this. Was Clark on good terms with his sergeants and the other men? the coroner pressed. Had they ever quarrelled with him about religion? Stevens claimed he had noticed no bad feeling. Another PC, Isaac Hickton, who had roomed with Clark at Stepney, corroborated Stevens's statement that Clark had broken open his own box. But he placed the disappearance of the PC much earlier on that fateful night. He usually met Clark at about eleven o'clock at Miller's Farm but, he now told the inquest jury, he had not turned up.

The coroner then informed his jury that 'certain information' had come to him and the police which would result in another adjournment—and probably the exhumation of the body. That caused a great ripple. What he mostly talked about later to Pearce, Superintendent Macquard, and Inspector Richardson, *The Times* was to reveal, was a letter which had been received from Bristol. Afterwards, the detectives were sent off in all directions.

Pearce asked a more recent member of the detective branch, the fair-haired, polite, and well-spoken Sergeant Kendall, who was 'a prodigious hand at pursuing private enquiries of a delicate nature',[2] to take Clark's colleagues with him when he went out on enquiries — in the hope that, in the circumstances of enforced familiarity, they might let something slip. Any reasonable expense, he was assured, would be met. Kendall (who had done good work on his own in a complicated case concerning anonymous threatening letters which themselves contained a poison, oxalic acid, which he discovered was used by the accused's father in his work of cleaning straw bonnets) found this new task rather hard going and the expenses unreasonable. He had been obliged to pay for all the refreshments, he complained later when trying to recoup his outgoings, 'Most of them having large families and, consequently, no money to spend'. He was also instructed to follow up every rumour — and there proved to be many. Most, he found, 'after walking a great many miles and at great expense . . . emanated only from idle, taproom talk'.

Sergeant Frederick Shaw was sent to the vicinity of Woburn and Evesham where, the ever-knowing *Times* revealed, 'the young women resides whom Clark was about to marry'. Shaw was to find out if there was any rival suitor who might have done the deed. He was the right man for the job. Charles Dickens was to describe him as 'a wiry little sergeant of meek demeanour and strong sense'. He would use this demeanour to advantage, Dickens claimed, by knocking at a door and asking 'a series of questions in any mild character you choose to prescribe to him, from charity boy upwards, and seem as innocent as an infant'. The result of his efforts, *The Times* continued, was to establish that the track pursued by Shackell in the Dagenham neighbourhood was the right one. The news-paper could say no more at the moment, for fear of prejudicing the ends of justice (a new sensitivity, this); but it was becoming obvious that jealousy and revenge, and not plunder, had been the motive.

'The vast excitement created by the horrible occurrence has not in the least degree diminished', exclaimed *The Times* when reporting on the attendance for the next inquest hearing. Intense interest was par for the course in murder cases, although the apparent involvement of the police themselves, together with the new factors that kept surfacing, may well have added piquancy to this particular one. Since the previous hearing, for

[2] Charles Dickens, 'The Detective Police'.

example, Clark's body had been exhumed, ostensibly to find any evidence of whether he had been shot. There was none, surgeons told the court, but they had found that the policeman's own cutlass fitted the major wounds.

The main drift of the evidence was still concerned with whether Parsons had been on duty throughout the night in question, and whether Kempton had in fact told Mrs Page that Parsons had not. Mrs Page stuck to her story and her daughter supported her, adding the allegation that Kempton had told them it was not the first time he had done duty for Parsons. A carpenter who had also shared the supper that evening said that he had not listened to the conversation, so could not help. Here the coroner interrupted, saying that when he had seen the witness the other day he had said he remembered Kempton saying he had done duty for Parsons on other occasions. The carpenter agreed he might have said this. 'Several of the jury', *The Times* reported, 'here expressed, very strongly, their opinion that this witness knew a great deal more than he seemed inclined to disclose.' A farm labourer who had helped remove the body now also denied having heard Kempton say he had done Parson's duty that night. A member of the jury, who happened to be the master of the witness, broke in to say that the man had told him many times that he *had* heard Kempton say it. The labourer was flummoxed; he admitted he had heard Kempton say he was on the horse that night, but claimed that Kempton had not said which part of the night.

Suddenly, it was all too much for Sergeant Parsons. 'I think the time has arrived when I should speak!' he broke in. It appeared that they were endeavouring to prove him the murderer, he complained, when he could produce several witnesses to contradict wholly the statements made. There was 'no imputation whatever' as to his involvement, the coroner insisted. The court was merely trying to discover whether or not Kempton had made the statement. Parsons should be pleased that they were going to such trouble 'to sift the matter', as it was in his interest that they did so.

Next, a local grocer said that Kempton had claimed to him that he was on the horse during the night in question and had kept it out as long as he dared. Then the sergeant's sister, Julia Parsons, told how she had seen her brother and PC Clark together — *on the night of the murder*. She and Mrs Parsons had been going home from Romford across the fields at about nine o'clock when they had seen Parsons on his horse and Clark walking beside him. 'The deceased', she declared, 'appeared to be in very good spirits. My brother's wife expressed that she was very tired and the deceased offered jokingly to put her on my brother's horse.' After describing this touching

97

domestic scene, Julia Parsons went on the give her brother an alibi. He had come home at around midnight, she admitted—to make out the report—but had gone out again before one o'clock and had not got back until nine o'clock that morning.

When Parsons got his chance, he produced first the landlord of the Cross Keys public house who testified to serving him with a pint of porter while he was on duty at midnight, then a carter who said he seen Parsons on horseback when passing through Dagenham between three and four in the morning. The coroner accepted that Parsons must have been on duty all night; the question was whether Kempton had made the statement to the contrary to Mrs Page. The evidence seemed to point that way, though why he had said it God only knew. Where exactly had *she* been on the night of the murder? he had asked Mrs Page when she gave evidence. She had previously said she had been in the bedroom, but had she not told a neighbour she had actually been sitting up all night in the kitchen while her husband was in the barn 'watching his corn' (in case it was stolen or set alight)? The neighbour was produced, and agreed that, when she had asked Mrs Page whether she had heard any cries for help that night, the farmer's wife had insisted she had not, even though she had been in the kitchen all night.

Another witness, Mrs Elizabeth Dodd, claimed to have actually seen Clark with his probable murderer on the night of his death. She had been walking back from London where she had been 'after a place' when, at about eleven o'clock, she crossed the Dagenham fields. 'In a second cornfield' she spotted a tall man in a fustian coat who was asking a policeman the time. 'He then used improper language to him. I was very frightened, as there was someone looking over the hedge.' When she got near Romford, said Mrs Dodd, she met two girls who asked her if she had heard some screams. She had seen the tall man before, several times, 'sitting in the fields near Mr Lee's, eating bread with a very large knife'. This sensational evidence did not entirely deflect attention from the police. Before the end of the hearing, Kempton again denied having said he had done Parson's duty. The outspoken jury expressed their conviction that he had, and the coroner wound up the proceedings by informing them that Superintendent Pearce had told him that keeping the inquest open would not only aid the police but further the cause of justice. Therefore, he would adjourn it for another month.

In the interim, the reward, which had finally been offered after the second hearing, began to produce results. The decade was not called 'the hungry forties' for nothing.

8

VERY ACTIVE OFFICERS

THE TWELFTH OF AUGUST 1846, the opening of the game-shooting season, was a bad day for the sport due, said *The Times*, to 'the late storms'. It was bad day, too, for Dennis Flinn, John Hennessy, and Eileen Rankin. On that date they were brought before Ilford magistrates on suspicion of murdering P C Clark. In attendance were Macquard, Richardson, Pearce, and 'some officers of the detective police'. Giving evidence against the accused were two fellow labourers, Michael Welch and Felix Sweeney. Welch, who spoke first, had left an Ireland in the grip of the potato famine and in the six subsequent months had taken casual farm work wherever he could find it. His fourth hiring was to a farm in Kent where, during a lull in the harvesting, fellow worker Eileen Rankin had explained that she and Flinn had no need to be there. Flinn had been earning good money near London until he had assaulted a policeman and so was forced to flee into the country. Pressed for details, she added that it had been on account of an Irishman who had come into a room where they had been drinking and had started to sing. The locals had objected, and a mêlée had ensued. A police sergeant on horseback had arrived and had been struck by a stone. Then Flinn and Hennessy had assaulted another policeman, *who was found dead in a field in the morning*.

Eileen Rankin now denied ever telling this rambling story and, of course, Flinn and Hennessy denied ever having committed a murder. Indeed, they appeared stunned and horrified by the situation in which they found themselves. Rankin had promised police that she would tell all, but after Flinn was overheard muttering to her that she should keep her mouth shut, she retracted. The police were heartened to find in her bag two white gloves 'of the type policeman wore', but she insisted they had been given her by someone at St Mary Cray in Kent.

Police told the magistrate that they had dispatched officers in various directions, hunting for further information, and they would be back soon. Could the case be adjourned for two or three hours? Or the accused remanded? The magistrate chose a week's remand, whereupon Hennessy burst into tears saying, 'That boy [Welch] is taking my life away!' In fact, he had no need to worry because Kendall, during the week that followed, was able to confirm that Hennessy and Flinn were elsewhere at the pertinent time—and another sensational development had led off in yet another direction.

Rumour was rife, *The Times* reported on 18 August, that several Dagenham policeman had been arrested by Superintendent Pearce and the detective police on a charge of murder. But the newspaper had ascertained that, while this was true in some respects, what had actually happened was that P C Butfoy had taken himself off to Scotland Yard, where he spilled a considerable quantity of beans to the effect that all the evidence given by police at the inquest had been untrue.

In fact, the officers (Hickton, Kempton, Farnes, Butfoy, and Parsons) had not been arrested, merely suspended from duty, and at the next inquest hearing, held in the half-timbered Cross Keys inn, they duly made their appearance, wearing 'private clothes'.

P C Butfoy was called first, and confessed that he had lied. He had not seen the sergeant that night, but Parsons had asked him to say that he had, as they were 'all in a mess' and must stick together. Now, he revealed that *he himself* had not been on duty at all. He recounted how both he and Parsons had attended the police court in the morning and had then got drunk together. So drunk, in fact, that the sergeant had excused him duty that night. He could give no assistance as to the the death of Clark but added, lethally, 'only it looks strange that the sergeant does not account for his time from half past nine o'clock until eleven and that Clark was not seen by a man who was invariably in the habit of seeing him at eleven o'clock at the Four Wants.'

P Cs Farnes, Kempton, and Hickton also confessed to lying previously. Kempton admitted that he had taken over the sergeant's duty at midnight; he was supposed to meet Clark shortly afterwards at the Four Wants, but the young P C had not appeared. Farnes retracted his claim to have seen Parsons that night—adding that the sergeant had written down the time he had to say, as he had done for the others. Farnes also confessed that Kempton had asked him to stick to his story that he had seen *him* (Kempton) at six o'clock—which he had not. Parsons's cool response, when it was pointed out that his colleagues now claimed he was not on duty that night, was a simple 'They have sworn falsely.' As for the allegations that he had written down what times they should say, 'The case was that my superintendent called on me to account for my time, and I put it down on paper for the men, as they contradicted each other.'

'They all contradict *you*', the coroner pointed out.

'I can't help that', he retorted.

Next, a farm labourer named Luke White described how he had seen P C Clark at around ten-thirty on the night in question. He had been getting his master's wagon 'ready for potatoes' when the P C came walking along, singing a hymn to himself, and enquiring how he had toiled the day away. White replied that he had had a very long one. Clark looked in his pockets for a tract he had brought for him but could not find it, so he left, promising to wake the labourer up between 3 and 4 a.m., as he had done on other occasions. But (obviously) he never arrived. A porter named Henry Clements directed suspicion back to Parsons. He claimed to have seen the sergeant sitting in a public bar engrossed in a newspaper, murmuring, 'Poor fellow, I wish I had not done it now.' At that, he had jumped up and said, 'Done what?', but the sergeant did not reply. Since then, said Clements, Kempton had threatened him and told him to say nothing.

'The place is full of the detective force', exclaimed *The Times* after another adjournment, 'and the suspended policemen are under their strict surveillance; and so great is the suspicion attached to the sergeant, that Messrs Kendall, Langley, and Shaw, have received positive instructions not to permit him out of their sight, and to take care that no communication whatever takes place between him and the other constables.'

Kendall, however, was soon hot on another trail, following a lead somehow overlooked by the *Times* sleuths. They had discovered another woman in the life of the upstanding P C Clark: one Susan Perry, whom he had met when at Arbour Square and had seen since at Dagenham. What was more, when Kendall found her and brought her in for questioning, they learned that she had a husband who, although the couple had been separated for two years, remained very jealous. To cap it all, James Perry had been seen in the Dagenham area on the night of the murder — leaving a public house with three other men.

James Perry was instantly elevated to the position of suspect number one and Kendall sent to look for him. He found him working for a cement manufacturer in Dartford, across the river from Dagenham, but there proved to be absolutely no hard evidence against him. One of the lesser-known detective-sergeants, Edward Langley, who had been in the department for only 18 months, was instructed to get into Perry's company. He did so, on several occasions, but failed to extract any damaging admissions.

He was sent on to Becontree Heath to make some enquiries about Mr Palmer, the man who had found Clark's hat, and who happened to have just committed suicide. But poor Langley did not have much luck there either.

Meanwhile, Kendall had spent three days tracing a cabman who had claimed to have carried 'two gents who were tipsy and covered with blood' away from a spot near the East India Dock (the next dock up-river from Dagenham) on the night of the murder. This trail, too, led nowhere.

It was an exhausting interlude for the Branch. Just getting from Westminster to Dagenham and back involved taking a horse bus to the railway station (6*d*.), a train to Romford (1/9*d*. 2nd class), then a 'fly' from Romford station to Dagenham (£3, 'there being no other conveyance'). Alternatively they took a horse bus all the way which, though cheaper, took much longer and was considerably less comfortable. Such journeys made for long days and little home life. Of course, many nights had to be spent away. Kendall, when submitting his expenses, totalled his nights in lodgings as 39, 18 of these being outside the Metropolitan Police district (the expense rates being different).

By now, rumours were rife that Parsons would come out of the final inquest hearing charged with murder. The excitement caused by 'the Dagenham murder' was getting out of hand. The Detective Branch, living up to expectations yet again, produced a fresh police witness, P C George Dunning, who recollected that, on the night of 27 August last, he had heard Parsons and his sister quarrelling 'upstairs' (presumably in the sergeant's quarters). She had accused the sergeant of something. 'Do you mean this affair?' Parsons had asked. 'Yes, this affair and others too', she had replied. At this point Parsons had begun to cry and P C Dunning had heard no more. But when the coroner pressed him, he admitted hearing the sergeant threaten to throw his sister downstairs if she did not hold her tongue. He had reported this to Sergeant Pearson at Dagenham police station. He had also, the coroner reminded him, reported hearing Julia Parsons say, 'You know you are guilty of it.'

'No, I did not report the word "guilty" that I recollect', said Dunning.

'You must recollect either one thing or the other', exclaimed the coroner, ' and if you do not you are the most unfit person to give evidence before this or any other jury!'

Julia Parsons admitted to the quarrel but claimed that it concerned family matters, and that Clark's death had never been mentioned.

Summing up, the coroner said the motive must have been one of revenge, due to the terrible injuries inflicted. In his opinion, both Parsons and Butfoy were still lying, and the jury must make up their minds whether there was enough evidence to bring in a verdict of wilful murder against any person. Where *were* both men that night? After a harangue about the 'wilful and corrupt perjury' of the policemen, about which 'there were no words strong enough in the English language to express the disgust which must be felt by all right-minded persons', he cleared the court so that the jury could deliberate. They came to the conclusion that it was wilful murder committed by some person or persons unknown and, as *The Times* put it, 'the proceedings in this protracted and truly mysterious affair then terminated'. But, of course, they hadn't.

Once again, Pearce suffered allegations of shady practices, or at least of complicity in some of those which may have occurred. The coroner's brother, one Reverend Lewis, told the *Times* reporter that a bloody handkerchief, found in a field by Sergeant Langley when returning to search the scene with Parsons, had been planted there by police themselves 'in order to mislead the investigation'. He claimed that Superintendent Pearce was aware of this, but was covering up, and if no one else would bring such conduct before the public, he certainly would.

This, understandably, drew an aggrieved report to the Yard from Pearce — which resulted in a note on the file suggesting that, because of the apparent grounds for unfavourable opinions of the police in this case, it would be inadvisable to take any steps on this report. Sir William Somerville, Under Secretary at the Home Office, agreed, adding. 'I have explained to Supt. Pearce and that of course it is not for him to chat to the Commissioners of such an accusation.' 'Put with the other papers on the Dagenham case' was the final cryptic comment. The Dagenham file continued to grow.

One anonymous but emphatic letter-writer thought there was no question but that smugglers were involved, and that they could only operate with the connivance of the police. The religious PC Clark had probably refused to join them 'in these doings', so 'it was considered by all parties the best plan to put him out of the way'. The smugglers had done the deed but the police were privy to it, 'which accounts thoroughly for their infamous conduct throughout the whole business'. A terse note on the file commented that there was no evidence to support the smugglers theory.

Another letter, from a Bristol address, was signed by a Mr Bragg who, he believed, had some valuable information and wanted to know whether he could give it without bringing his name before the public at present.

Would they write and tell him? They did better, they sent the ever-mobile Kendall post-haste to see him. But the Mr Bragg resident at the Bristol address denied all knowledge of the letter and promptly wrote another, not only to confirm this, but also to demonstrate how dissimilar was his handwriting.

Kendall was also sent to re-interview Mrs Dodd, 'the female who made the rambling statement before the coroner' about a policeman talking to a man wearing fustian trousers and another looking over a hedge. She, too, now denied everything. She had not seen the incident; she did not know the fields in question; she had not even been living in the area at the time; and it had been a fortnight after the murder when she had walked to London after a place. Her whole story, she admitted, had been 'imagination'. 'I find', commented Kendall wearily, 'she is a person of bad character and is considered by many in Romford to be of unsound mind.'

Meanwhile, Sergeant Parsons's wife died, under what a local paper described as 'melancholy circumstances'. She had recently given birth, and 'her husband's situation in this horrid affair' had played on her mind and 'accelerated her death'. There were more deaths to come, but for the moment the numerous murder leads had come to naught.

Seven weeks after the inquest verdict, it was announced that charges of perjury could not be sustained again Farnes, Stevens, and Butfoy, as they had not been sworn when first examined, but that they were to be instantly dismissed from the force. It must have come as no surprise in March of the following year that the main prosecution witnesses were these three discharged officers. A true bill was found against Parsons, Hickton, and Kempton for conspiracy to pervert the course of justice, but only against Kempton and Hickton for perjury — as it was felt that such a charge against Parsons could not be sustained. They were to go for trial at the summer assize. A formal hearing was arranged at the end of March for them to apply for bail. Only Kempton turned up for this little ceremony — Parsons and Hickton had fled.

Nothing was heard of them for several months (which Kempton spent in custody, unable to find the £400 surety). The trial had been scheduled for 14 July; lo and behold, on 30 June, Hickton was brought to Arbour Square police station by a Sergeant Harvey of the Derby police — an old school-friend of his — after having been handed over by his own father. When Hickton had heard about the rewards offered for his capture, he knew it was only a matter of time. His response was to go home and persuade his father to inform on him to Sergeant Harvey — so that both could share the reward. Not surprisingly, senior policeman voiced doubts over the validity of such a reward claim, but forwarded the request to the Home Office with the information that Joseph Hickton was a very poor man. It was decreed that Joseph Hickton and Sergeant Harvey should receive £25 between them—riches when one considers that a policeman's pay was only £1 a week.

Kempton and Hickton were found guilty and sentenced to seven years' transportation. The trial also renewed interest in the missing Parsons. The governor of Windsor gaol thought he had him in custody, and Sergeant Whicher was sent down to look at the man. But Parsons it was not. Whicher decided the man was probably a deserter, and the reason he had hesitated when accused of being Parsons was that he was unsure which was the lesser of the two evils. (The treatment of deserters was harsh.)

Parsons, in fact, was doing what a great many fugitives did at the time, labouring on the new railway lines, and he was eventually tracked down near Grimsby by Sergeant Fork and P C Barnes of the Metropolitan Police. Suddenly, the murder case itself emerged from the doldrums when a tiny envelope, addressed to Superintendent Pearce and inscribed 'to be instantly placed in his hands', was delivered to Bow Street police station. It came from a Mr Blairblock of Romford, who said that shortly after the murder a labourer had found a bloody smock frock, jacket, and trousers, which had been thrown over a hedge onto a pile of night soil near Kempton's cottage. Unable to get them clean enough to make use of, the labourer had buried the clothes. The writer said he would meet a particular train to Romford the following morning, in case Pearce should 'want some conversation' with him. He'd wait for the next train along as well, he said, adding cryptically, 'Ralph Page died on Monday last, under great suspicion of death by laudanum.'

The well-spoken Sergeant Kendall was sent down to have some conversation with Mr Blairblock. After extensive enquiry it was found that the clothes had been buried in a gravel pit and would require a great deal of digging out, particularly since the labourer did not remember the exact spot 'to within three roods'. In any case, the pits were very wet and the clothes likely to have rotted away. That line of enquiry was abandoned.

The inquest jury on Ralph Page brought in an open verdict. They had heard evidence that one of his ribs had been broken—probably during an election brawl in Romford—and that he had taken some laudanum after complaining of 'a great pain' in his chest, but that it was possible he might have died of apoplexy. He had had two previous attacks, and on this occasion had been in a state of excitement brought on by his daughter's wedding the previous day.

Interest was again revived when a soldier in custody at Chatham confessed to the murder. Pearce and Kendall went down to interview him. He told them that he and three other men ('new acquaintances') had been poaching hares and rabbits when Clark had caught them. 'Game not in season at this time', commented Charles Rowan in a margin note to this report, 'nor likely to be shot in cornfields and at night.' By then Kendall had talked to the man's relatives, who revealed that he had been mentally unstable since suffering from smallpox in his youth. Pearce also thought it likely he had come up with this tale to save himself from the punishment he would get at court martial, 'this being his fifth time of desertion'.

It was to be March 1848 before Parsons was eventually brought to trial. The case was halted by Lord Justice Denman, who held that the sergeant had not been conspiring to defeat the ends of justice but merely to screen himself from a neglect of duty charge.

Kempton had not yet left for Van Diemen's Land,[1] but was incarcerated in one of those death traps, a prison hulk, moored at Woolwich. His father now petitioned the Home Office, asking that he should not be transported. An attached reports points out that Kempton had been in the police for six years and had had 'only one report for neglect of duty.' The following October, Kempton's father tried again. Superintendent Pearce, when asked for his comments, was of the opinion that the man was no more culpable than Hickton, who not only had had his sentenced commuted but had since been discharged from prison. The commissioners agreed that Kempton should be similarly treated. His release marked the end (for the time being) of this 'protracted and truly mysterious affair'.

It was Sergeant Kendall's stamina and pocket which had most felt the strain of this lengthy enquiry but Inspector Shackell's veins had not fared well either. Certainly, by August 1848 they were in a very bad state. 'Ulcerated and diseased' is how a sympathetic Richard Mayne described them to the Home Office when trying to get a decent pension for him. The foundation for the trouble had been laid when Shackell was kicked in the legs several years earlier, the commissioner explained, and long continuous duty since then had finished them off—'a common consequence'. There was much contention, due to the fact that Shackell had not served the requisite 15 years to qualify for an ill-health pension (only 13 years, 1

---

[1] Due to overcrowding in the colony, the first third of transportation sentences were being served in British prisons.

month, and 4 days), although with his Bow Street service taken into account it totalled almost 19. Had he been a Bow Street patrol or officer, and not gaoler, that service would have counted. The Home Office were anxious not to set precedents, but eventually the commissioners seem to have done quite well for Shackell.

That same year there was another Chartist scare, and, as with Runner Goddard and Shackell in 1839, Inspector Haynes and Sergeant Thornton were sent north to gather intelligence, a job which included keeping an eye on Chartists drilling in Halifax. There is no doubt they were thereby acting as 'political spies', but this time there were no terrible consequences, as there had been in 1833, when P C Culley was murdered by a crowd who were incensed by Sergeant Popay's undercover activities.

To replace Shackell, Inspector Field was brought into the Branch — just in time for what some considered to be the department's biggest case yet.

9

WONDROUS INVENTIONS

IT WAS A HARD LIFE being one of Scotland Yard's first detectives, but it was an interesting one. Charles Dickens observed that members of the Branch gave the impression of being men 'habitually leading lives of strong mental excitement'. Nevertheless, despite such constant stimulation, they presented a picture of respectability and good deportment, he discovered when he met some of them in 1850. There was nothing 'lounging or slinking' in their manners. They were keenly observant, quick of perception, showed unusual intelligence, and had 'good eyes', with which they looked you full in the face when they spoke.

These paragons, when not employed on special cases, covered a great deal of ground. They attended every notable event, from Jenny Lind's final appearance to agricultural shows — any location which attracted the crowds and hence 'the swell mob'. Epsom Races was a regular date in their calendar, particularly Derby Day. The powers the Detective Branch enjoyed there would be the envy of today's police employed on football or carnival crowd control. They simply waited at the railway station for the swell mob to arrive, then packed them off home again. Afterwards, they went to the track to pick up the thieves and tricksters who had slipped through their net.

Apart from picking pockets, the swell mob indulged in confidence tricks such as 'thimble-rigging' (a sharping trick with three thimbles and a pea) and 'gammoning a countryman' (conning a simple rural fellow out of money by, for example, pretending to get him a job). Those arrested were popped into a portable prison, much like a gypsy caravan and dubbed 'Colonel Rowan's Cage' by the *Illustrated London Life*. What would villains of days gone by have made of this 'Epsomic lock-up', the journal mused. 'Barrington, Bill Soames or Jack Shepherd had never been clapped into that carriage for convicts or post chaise for pickpockets by Hughes,[1] or the wily Thornton.'

[1] Probably Inspector Samuel Hughes of A Division.

Of course, the detectives also did a great deal of travelling when following their suspects or being called in to assist on cases outside London. This must have been a mixed blessing, given the fact that in many ways transport was still quite primitive. Even the faster, newfangled steam train, particularly in the second-class (in which police usually travelled) and third-class coaches, had hard seats and open sides, so that passengers' eyes were filled with smuts. In winter they were very cold, and when it rained passengers were forced to sit in a puddle. Ordinary citizens could also have their dignity affronted, claimed *Punch*, by having to sit next to 'a ragamuffin in handcuffs with a policeman next to him'. Then there was always the danger of the boiler bursting and killing the traveller en route.

However, the trains were a big step up from the post chaise, which was still in use where trains and the new omnibuses had not yet ventured. (Charles Dickens was given to pondering how many months of incessant travelling in a post chaise it would take to kill a man). None the less, the constant changes of venue must have been stimulating for the detectives, particularly when they were called upon to continue their pursuit all the way across the Atlantic, as Thornton did when chasing an Irish bank robber in 1847.

It must also have been companionable to belong to a select group who shared fame and unusual adventures, and who also had individual experiences to share later. Dickens was also impressed by the detectives' lack of self-centredness, noting how they praised each other's accomplishments and encouraged each other to tell a special tale.

Dickens met the detectives just after what many regard as their biggest case up to that time, and one in which all eight of the branch were involved. In charge were Inspector John Haynes (who had now seen two other senior officers come and go) and the portly and husky-voiced Inspector Field, past master of self-publicity. Their sergeants were the pock-marked Jonathan Whicher, a single man whose thoughtfulness gave the impression that he was engaged in deep arithmetical calculations; the middle-aged and ruddy-faced Stephen Thornton, 'famous for steadily pursuing the inductive process' or, as the *Illustrated London Life* would have it, 'wily'; the wiry and innocent-looking Frederick Shaw; the fair-haired, polite, but not docile Edward Kendall; smooth-faced Henry Smith, with his 'strange air of simplicity'; and Edward Langley, a man of 19 years' service, the last four spent in the detective department, whose previous experience was to prove vital.

The case was not so much a mystery to be solved by the department, as the victim's friends quickly pointed the way to the suspects, but more a chase worthy of the Bow Street Runners — a chase updated by the speed with which the ever-expanding railway system allowed suspects to put a great distance between themselves and the scene of the crime, and by the use of another, newer, invention by the police which closed that gap even more quickly.

The culprits were identified very early on by alert members of the public — in particular one Mr Flynn. On a Friday afternoon in August 1849, Flynn confided to a PC Wright of M or Southwark Division that Patrick O'Connor, his cousin and colleague in the London Dock customs department at Wapping, had not been to work that day — nor was he to be found at his lodgings off the Mile End Road. Flynn asked the constable to accompany him to the residence for which O'Connor was last seen heading, 3, Minver Place, on the opposite side of the river in Bermondsey. He knew that the lady of the house had invited the missing exciseman to supper and it was she, a handsome, well-dressed, 30-year-old with a slight French accent, who answered the door to them.

Yes, she knew O'Connor was missing, she told them, and it surprised her, for he was a man of such regular habits. Yes, she had expected him for dinner the previous evening but he had never arrived. She had gone to his lodgings to seek him out and had been even more surprised not to find him there. In fact, the last she had seen of him was on Wednesday night when he had left her house 'very tipsy'. The 50-year-old O'Connor, a gauger of exciseable liquor casks, had still not surfaced by the Sunday, and his friends and colleagues were becoming increasingly concerned. They issued handbills offering a reward of £10 for any information, and two of them, Mr Keating and Mr Graham, also called on the lady with the accent, Maria Manning. She seemed somewhat nervous on this occasion, but (apparently) equally puzzled by the absence of the family friend.

Mr Flynn also called again that day in the company of a plain-clothes policeman, PC Henry Barnes of the K or Stepney Division. He was the PC who had helped capture Sergeant Parsons, and was probably one of Pearce's divisional detectives, since the Press referred to him as an 'active officer' — a term used for plain-clothes detectives. Flynn and Barnes got no reply. They met with Mr Keating and Mr Graham, and all four took themselves off to Stones End police station, the headquarters of M or Southwark Division. There they asked for watch to be kept on the Mannings' house, and for the services of PC Wright to study Mrs Manning's countenance whilst she was being questioned by Flynn the following day. Flynn and

Wright found Maria in, but extracted little from her but murmurings about 'poor O'Connor' and opinions that the family friend tended to be erratic in his behaviour — as well as an impression that she was beginning to look somewhat flurried and indisposed. Mr Manning, as previously, was unavailable. (The previous visit by Flynn and Wright on the Friday before was never mentioned in Press reports after the first police court hearing, and it is possible that the Press had confused it with the Monday visit.)

O'Connor had remarkably persistent relatives and friends, although their concern may not have been totally altruistic. It was common knowledge that O'Connor's money-lending activities had rendered him quite wealthy, and he possessed, among other things, a great many French railway shares. Mrs Manning admitted having visited the missing man's lodgings at least twice since his disappearance and, more importantly, having been allowed to stay alone in his room — but that was no more than she had done many times before. Finally, Flynn broke open O'Connor's boxes, only to find them empty of anything of consequence.

The following day, after further agitation from friends, police were to find 3 Minver Place in the same condition — empty. In fact, all a PC Burton reported finding in the flagstoned kitchen were 28 pieces of newly washed linen and a shovel, and, in the small garden which led off the kitchen, an assortment of shrubs and some scarlet runners tied up with string.

Meanwhile, more details of the relationship between the Mannings and O'Connor were emerging. O'Connor, it transpired, had been a suitor of Maria's when she was personal maid to Lady Blantyre, but had been ousted by the younger Frederick Manning who seemed to have better prospects. Although only a guard on the Great Western Railway, he had told Maria he had great expectations of inheritance from his mother, and persuaded her that he also had ways of getting more money. He had, but was fired when he put them into practice, the GWR objecting to the fact that money kept going missing from his train. He tried his hand at keeping a public house in Taunton, but when a bullion raid took place on the GWR the pair were suspected of being involved and arrested. They were released owing to lack of evidence (others involved were transported) but the bad publicity ruined business and they ended up running a beer-house in the Hackney Road. A disgruntled Maria, who had merely wished to escape from service into an easier life, then discovered that O'Connor was in fact quite wealthy. They resumed contact — and their affair, he becoming a 'family friend' and regular visitor to their rented accommodation at 3 Minver Place.

Police handling of the case so far had been scarcely sparkling, and it was another three days before PCs Burton and Barnes were to dig up the garden and give the flat a more thorough search. Back in the basement kitchen, Barnes now noticed that some of the mortar between the flagstones was damp in places. 'This arrested my attention', he was to report, without irony. His attention was further arrested by the sight he saw on removing some of the flagstones and digging down a bit — the naked body of a man embedded, face down, in unslaked lime.

The corpse proved to have a bullet in the brain and extensive fractures to the back of the skull. Despite the fact that the body was fast disintegrating, as it was intended to do in the lime, Mr Flynn quickly identified it by its very long jaw bone and the fine set of false teeth retrieved from the mouth. It was Patrick O'Connor, and the murder hunt was on.

The following day, Barnes and Burton informed the coroner that they had the case well in hand, which seems to have been something of an overstatement given their performance so far. They were sure that, if given time, they could procure most important evidence, they told him. They had a lead towards this already, and would appreciate a week's adjournment to get more. What good was evidence, the coroner might have replied, when the chief suspects had been allowed to escape? On the wanted posters subsequently rushed out, Frederick Manning sounded quite unlovely, with his stout figure, florid complexion, full, bloated face, small, sandy whiskers, and 'peculiar fall of eyelids at the corners'. Maria received kinder treatment, as befitted her developing role as femme fatale. With her long dark hair and a fresh complexion, she was described as being 'good looking' and dressing 'very smartly'. But as well as her striking appearance, Maria had two identifying factors which must have gladdened the hearts of the policemen: her accent, and a facial scar running from the right side of her chin towards her neck. Any information about these two suspects, the posters announced, was to be passed to Inspector Field of the Detective Branch at Scotland Yard.

There was a distinct possibility that Maria had headed for her native country, where she would be less obvious. The commissioners immediately wrote to the British consuls in Le Havre, Calais, Dieppe, and Boulogne, asking them to keep their eyes open, and sent Inspector Field and Sergeant Whicher to France. The police there, reported the *Morning Chronicle*, 'rendered them every possible assistance' by searching Parisian hotels and lodging houses and keeping watch at railway stations. The Atlantic remained a popular escape route, and a crossings timetable had been found on the Mannings mantelpiece; no one was surprised at the news that two persons by the name of Manning had boarded the *SS Victoria*, an American packet-ship which had left London docks on the very day the body was found.

Sergeants Langley and Thornton were already searching ships at Portsmouth when they received a message from Inspector Haynes that the *SS Victoria* was due to pass Portland Bill and that they must get it stopped. But despite their efforts, the ship failed to respond to signals instructing it to heave to. The detectives appealed to the Royal Navy, who graciously provided them with a high-speed steam yacht, the *Fire Queen*, in which to give chase. Four and a half hours after leaving Portsmouth, Sergeants Langley and Thornton boarded the passenger ship, but, reported *The Times*, 'the fugitives were not discovered' — just a Mrs Rebecca Manning, who did not answer Maria's description, and her daughter.

According to the Press, it was Sergeant Shaw of the Detective Police who finally pulled the rabbit out of the hat. His enquiries in the Mannings' neighbourhood revealed that Mrs Manning had left 3 Minver Place, alone and in a great hurry, on the afternoon of Monday, 13 August. She had taken a cab, onto which were piled several of her large boxes and her carpet bag. Shaw tracked down Kirk, driver of Hackney cab No. 1186, who revealed that it was he who had driven the lone Maria — to London Bridge railway station. They had stopped en route so that she could buy some white cards to attach to the larger of the boxes, announcing, 'Mrs Smith, passenger to Paris, to be left till called for', before depositing them in London Bridge left-luggage office. Then the cabman had taken her on to Euston station.

Inspector Haynes immediately obtained access to the boxes, which contained clothing, including a bloodstained[2] dress, labelled as belonging to Maria de Roux (Mrs Manning's maiden name), and letters from O'Connor. Having made sure 'Mrs Smith' was his quarry, he sped on to Euston Station, where he discovered that a woman answering Mrs Manning's description and with luggage marked 'Mrs Smith' had taken a train for Edinburgh on the previous Monday.

To give instant personal chase was no longer always necessary, now that

---

[2] Police in those days quite happily referred to items as 'bloodstained' just on the evidence of their eyes, but in fact the chemical test used then, as was admitted by the chemist in this case, was a negative one (of elimination of other possibilities such as fruit stains) rather than a positive.

the police could make use of the electric telegraph. Introduced in 1836, its use had spread rapidly with the growth of the railways, and the very first such linkage — between Paddington and Slough stations — proved crucial to the capture of a murderer, John Tawell, in 1845. (After committing his crime in Slough, he was seen leaving on a Paddington-bound train. This intelligence was telegraphed ahead, and railway police were waiting at the other end. However, they followed Tawell rather than picking him up and, indeed, lost him; but with the aid of a Metropolitan Police inspector they were reunited and an arrest was made.)

By 1849, about a third of the railway network was linked by the electric telegraph. Inspector Haynes had used it to give instructions to Langley and Thornton about stopping the *SS Victoria*, and now it was employed to flash Mrs Manning's details to Superintendent Moxey, head of Edinburgh Police. 'Mr Haynes had scarcely arrived at Scotland Yard on his return' reported *The Times*, 'when a messenger from the Telegraph Office reached there, bearing intelligence that Maria Manning had been arrested.' Another telegraph swiftly followed, giving details of some of the property found on Maria, which included banknotes known to have been issued on O'Connor's cheques two days after he had disappeared, and railway share certificates, some of which she had foolishly tried to sell.

The capture had been made 'thanks to the energy and activity of our detective force in the first instance, and secondly to the great invention of the age — the electric telegraph', said the *Morning Chronicle*. The great invention was also much used by the Press to keep the public up to date on the progress of the case — such reports being invariably headed: '(BY ELECTRIC TELEGRAPH)'. The complex manner in which speeded-up communications were affecting the pursuit of criminals was illustrated by *The Times*' electric telegraph report, datelined 'Edinburgh, Tuesday', giving details of Moxey's capture of Mrs Manning:

> he was shown into a room, in which he found a well-dressed woman reading a copy of *The Times* newspaper of the 20th inst., which gives an account of the murder and a description of the parties supposed to have committed it.

(Edinburgh police were to allege that they had not received such a description by police channels, and had had to resort to the one in *The Times*.) Sometimes the police were criticized for not putting the new invention to greater use. The *Morning Chronicle*, claiming that police had expected Mrs Manning to arrive at Euston two days after her arrest and had turned up there to meet her, commented: 'it is strange that the Electric Telegraph was not called into action to set this matter right.'

The case was, of course, causing a tremendous sensation. The 'immense crowds' which had gathered around Minver Place during the first couple of days had now dwindled, and only a 'stray idler' put in an appearance. Instead, the multitude were gathering expectantly around Scotland Yard and meeting every possible train arriving at Euston from Edinburgh. (Some historians put this intense interest in crime down to the lack of cheap public entertainment.) In the event, the protagonists (Superintendent Moxey, Mrs Manning, and Edinburgh City Criminal Officers Milligan and Fallon) were to arrive at 4.45 a.m. on the Thursday morning, after a 17½-hour journey. All had travelled first class — a fact which was to raise eyebrows at the Yard.

Those hours closeted with Mrs Manning were to have a profound effect on the policemen who had escorted her. The first hint of this was given when Superintendent Moxey, on being told by the magistrate that he need not remain in London while waiting for the next hearing but that he must keep Mrs Manning's property in his care, asked if he might speak to her, as she had expressed a strong desire to see him before he left the capital. His request was granted, but the lady (who, *The Times* was at pains to point out, could not by any means be styled beautiful, as some papers had claimed) was probably put off by the pen, ink, and paper produced by an accompanying officer to record everything she said. Maria confined herself to claiming innocence of the crime. On the journey to London, Moxey was later to tell the court, she had confided in him that her husband was very violent towards her, and it was her terror of him which had made her take flight.

The Detective Branch had already gathered some formidable evidence to the contrary, indicating, moreover, that theirs was a totally premeditated crime. One of the most important witnesses was William Massey, a medical student, who had lodged with the suspects until 28 July, when Manning had asked him to leave, telling him that his elderly mother-in-law was coming to live with them. Previous to that, the apparently lonely Frederick Manning had confided in Massey that O'Connor was a wealthy man and, after getting into a state of intoxication (having been persuaded that port and brandy would help protect him against the cholera once again raging in the riverside areas), had willed much of it to Maria. But, more damningly, Manning had enquired of the medical student, in the course of their many conversations, what drugs would produce stupefaction but still enable a

115

man to put his hand to paper so that he could sign cheques; which was the most vulnerable part of the skull; whether an airgun made much noise when fired, and (laughingly, when discussing the waxwork figure of Rush[3]) whether a murderer could go to heaven. The medical student had recommended behind the ear as the place most usually attended by fatal results, and told Manning that, in his limited experience, airguns made little noise, but that murderers could not enter heaven.

Tradesmen had also started to remember that, on the day before the alleged murder, Maria Manning had purchased a strong shovel, and that in late July Frederick had ordered a bushel of unslaked lime 'for his garden'. The hunt for Frederick Manning was intensified. Before she took flight, Maria had sent Frederick out to sell their furniture. When he came back to find she had left, he soon followed suit — but where had he gone? Sightings were reported all over the country and abroad. Whicher, now back from France, was sent off to Plymouth to search an Australian emigrant ship, and a Constable Lockyer and Sergeant Langley (who had worked on the GWR theft case and knew Manning) ended up in Jersey. But, thought the Press, the west of England, Manning's home ground, was favourite. Men answering the suspect's description were apprehended from Dublin to John O'Groats. Among them was a Chelsea publican on a fishing trip to Wales with his brother. He was not only taken into custody, claimed *The Times*, but actually identified as Manning by a travelling salesman, who claimed to have known the suspect when he kept the pub in Taunton. The poor man was only released after Field had carried out some enquiries in Chelsea. The Jersey sighting proved the fruitful one, resulting in a candle-lit creep up darkened stairs by Langley, Lockyer, and local police officials. They caught Manning in bed at his lodgings. He immediately began to protest that it was all Maria's work. She had asked O'Connor to go downstairs to wash his hands before dinner, and at the foot of the stairs she had put one hand on his shoulder and shot him in the head with the other. Later, she had run out on him (Manning), taking all the loot. This fact was certainly borne out by the meagre goods in his solitary carpet-bag; a few worn clothes and seven pounds in gold. Maria had not only carried off all the money and stock but also the household linen (which she had left at London Bridge) and heaps of clothes and personal possessions. Superintendent Moxey's minions had their work cut out carefully logging it all. There were sarsnet (thin silk tissue) gowns, black silk stockings, piles of

---

[3] A double murderer hanged on 21 April 1849.

silks and satins, 'a piece of fancy gimp used as a mantilla', 'a volume of sacred poetry', and much, much more. One wonders what Moxey did with it all when ordered to keep it in his care — take it back to Edinburgh?

Even in the train to London from Southampton, Manning continued to tell Langley and Haynes about the crime, and to protest his innocence. But at this stage the exhausted Langley was falling asleep, and Haynes did most of the listening instead. Manning told him how afraid of his wife he was, and how it was she who had done the shooting. 'When I said it appeared by the papers that there were other wounds he made no reply to that,' the Inspector later told the court, 'but afterwards appeared to be low-spirited.' The purchase of the lime and the questions he had put to the medical student, Massey, had also made Manning's claims of innocence doutbful, to say the least, and new information gained shortly after his arrest revealed that he had also recently purchased a crowbar or 'ripping chisel' which was thought to have been used in the murder. This consolidated suspicions of his active and premeditated participation.

Both husband and wife, still blaming each other, were found guilty, and Manning eventually confessed to having finished off O'Connor with the ripping chisel on finding him still alive and moaning after Maria had shot him — 'I'd never liked him well.' Their public hanging, on 13 November 1847, was to attract the biggest crowds ever, estimated at between 30,000 and 50,000, and drew the condemnation of such spectacles from Charles Dickens, who attended none the less — though under protest. Maria is credited with instantly putting black satin out of fashion by wearing it for her execution.

It was confirmed that Criminal Officers Milligan and Fallon had actually travelled first class from Edinburgh, as they now claimed — Sergeant Sheppey, who met the train, had seen them alighting from the carriage, said Superintendent Pearce, who was given the task of looking into the large bill sent in by the Edinburgh Police.

The first-class fares claimed (£7 15s. return) were also correct according to Bradshaw's Railway Guide, and their expenses of £2 5s. each for the journey seemed reasonable. However, Superintendent Moxey's 'M & R' (meals and refreshment) claim of £2 3s. a day for ten days did not. After all, a Metropolitan police superintendent could only claim £1 7s. 6d. a day, and, estimating that Moxey earned 16s. 6d. a day, it was argued that he should be offered £1 13s. plus £1 for accommodation. 'Superintendent Moxey would thus receive double pay and so be guarded', wrote Pearce, 'against the probability of any stoppage being made from his salary at Edinburgh.'

But Moxey wanted no such protection, pointing out that Metropolitan superintendents were not in charge of their entire force as he was. He received 'a considerably higher salary than is paid to any of the Superintendents of the Metropolitan Police', and this M & R rate was what his commissioners allowed him when he came to London on police business. Among the many items the Scotsman had already claimed for was £15 to the Electric Telegraph Company, and fivepence for the purchase of a copy of the same issue of *The Times* which Mrs Manning had been reading when arrested. It gave the Edinburgh Police details of the suspects which, had they received copies of the Wanted notice, as they should have, they might not have needed.

As for the rewards: P C Lockyer and P C Harris of Edinburgh received £5 each, and Sergeants Shaw, Smith, Kendall, and Burton £8. Whicher, Langley, Barnes, and Thornton received £10 each, while Inspectors Haynes and Field received £15. Superintendent Moxey, however, received £30, which can't have gone down well south of the border. Neither, probably, did the compliments heaped upon Moxey by Mr Serjeant Wilkins, Mr Manning's defence counsel, who at the trial had congratulated Edinburgh on possessing such an excellent officer. Never, Wilkins declared, since he had been in the profession had he heard a man in Moxey's capacity give his evidence in so intelligent a manner and so creditably to himself. But Haynes, at least, may not have been too concerned, as he had just received another award for good service—promotion to superintendent.

A curious postscript to this case is offered by Charles Kingston in his book on famous trials, *The Bench and the Dock*,[4] in which he claims that Charles Dickens often discussed the trial, and had said that Maria Manning so charmed an elderly Scottish detective who helped escort her to London that he expressed his bitter regret at having taken part in the 'persecution' of a lady, and subsequently 'committed suicide in remorse'.

[4] Stanley Paul, 1925.

10

DICKENS AND
THE DETECTIVES

'IT IS A SULTRY EVENING at dusk. The stones of Wellington
Street are hot and gritty, and the watermen and the hackney-coachmen
at the Theatre opposite, are much flushed and aggravated. Carriages
are constantly setting down the people who have come to Fairyland;
and there is a mighty shouting and bellowing every now and then, deafening us for the moment, through the open windows.

So wrote the 38-year-old Charles Dickens as he set the scene for the
arrival, at the office of his new magazine, *Household Words*, of seven officers from 'the Detective Police' whom he had been given permission to
interview.

Of the original eight first detectives, only three remained: Sergeants
Whicher, Thornton, and Shaw. They were part of the group who settled
themselves in a semi-circle opposite 'the editorial sofa', accepting cigars
and a little (but not much) of the brandy from the circular table between.
The other two sergeants were Smith and Kendall.

The two inspectors sat at either end. One was Frederick Field—by now
'a middle-aged man of portly presence, with a large, moist, knowing eye, a
husky voice, and a habit of emphasising his conversation by the aid of a
corpulent finger, which is constantly in juxtaposition with his eyes or
nose'. (It is amusing to read in a body language picture caption in a 1989
Metropolitan Police recruiting advertisement: 'The man with his finger to
his nose is showing one of the signals associated with lying.')

Field and Smith had recently been called in on what was oddly termed a
'supposed murder' case: that of a woman servant, Sarah Snelling, found
dead on the kitchen floor of her master's house in Clapham, with a roll of
carpet under her head. There were signs of burglary, and her employer
claimed to have lost some plate—which police later found him using.
However, despite his odd behaviour—telling the police he had only
employed her because she was old and ugly and so he would not be
tempted, and murmuring as she was lowered into her grave, 'Ah poor girl,

A Division officers on duty at Epsom Races during the
1860s. From left to right: Inspector David Baldry, who
served at Buckingham Palace; Superintendent Robert
Walker, the man whom Charles Dickens mistook for a
detective; Inspector Eleazer Denning, who was in charge
of the parliamentary police; and PC Donald Swanson,
who was to lead the Jack the Ripper investigation and
become a superintendent.
(Courtesy of the Metropolitan Police)

she is gone, she will tell no tales' — he was not arrested, due mainly to lack of evidence, the cause of death never having been established.

The other inspector present in that office just off the Strand was a school-masterly Scotsman named Robert Walker. He was actually not a detective at all — although Dickens seems to have been unaware of this — but a member of Scotland Yard's Executive Branch. This department worked closely with the detectives and sometimes helped them out.

At a glance (according to the famous author), all of them took an inventory of the furniture and an accurate sketch of the editorial presence. 'The Editor feels that any gentleman in the company could take him up, if need should be, without the smallest hesitation, twenty years hence.' A bit of an exaggeration, perhaps, but one knows what he means about the eyes of policemen whipping round a room.

After the cigars had been lit, Dickens set the the ball rolling by 'a modest amateur reference' to the swell mob. Field, to his credit, immediately recommended Sergeant Whicher as London's greatest authority on this notorious group. One gets the feeling that when Dickens refers to Whicher's concise response, 'in well-chosen language', to the invitation to begin, he really means that Whicher was a little ponderous — as those who open the proceedings often tend to be. The others listened with great concentration and respect, and began chipping in only when the opportunity offered. Suddenly it was all very lively — but with the exact and statistical tone being maintained, not surprisingly, by Walker the 'admin' man.

> From these topics, we glide into a review of the most celebrated and horrible of the great crimes that have been committed within the last fifteen or twenty years. The men engaged in the discovery of almost all of them, and in the pursuit and apprehension of the murderers, are here, down to the very last instance. One of our guests gave chase to and boarded the emigrant ship, in which the murderess last hanged in London was supposed to have embarked. We learn from him that his errand was not announced to the passengers, who may have no idea of it to this hour. That he went below, with the captain, lamp in hand — it being dark, and the whole steerage abed and sea-sick — and engaged the Mrs Manning who *was* on board, in a conversation about her luggage until she was, with no small pains, induced to raise her head, and turn her face towards the light. Satisfied that she was not the object of his search, he quietly re-embarked in the Government steamer alongside, and steamed home again with the intelligence.

THE REAL THING

What struck Dickens most was that 'these brother officers only come in to the assistance of each other—not to the contradiction—and a more amicable brotherhood there could not be'. The tales they eventually told, on this occasion and on another visit (while making allowances for minor errors or exaggeration in the telling or reporting), give an idea of their work on other than murder cases, but also indicate how freely they assumed disguises and how they seemed to revel in the acting involved, and how much time and freedom of movement they had in following up one case, just like the Runners.

This is illustrated by Whicher's tale of the 'taking of Tally-ho Thompson . . . a famous horse stealer, couper and magsman',[1] which (after some prompting from his colleagues) he was persuaded to tell. Tally-ho was wanted for gammoning a countryman out of 'a good round sum of money, under pretence of getting him a situation—the regular old dodge' and for stealing a horse. Whicher was put on his trail, armed only with the information that Thompson's wife lived in Chelsea. He watched the house, particularly at post time, reckoning that her man would write to her. Sure enough, one morning the postman delivered a letter.

By talking to the postman and pretending he was a poor tradesman owed money by Thompson, Whicher discovered that the letter had contained money—probably a sovereign—but the postman was unable to remember the postmark. That, however, had been enough, Whicher told Dickens. He deduced that Mrs Thompson would want to let her husband know she had received the money safely, and his suspicions were confirmed when the little girl went out to buy writing paper, envelopes, and ink. When she came out of the house again, this time with the letter, he spoke to her (obviously, strangers showing an interest in children were not so suspect in those days) and, though unable to see the address, noticed that it was sealed with 'a kiss' (a drop of wax beside the seal). He introduced himself to the man in charge of the post office where it was posted, was permitted a look at the letter thus sealed, and found it was addressed to a Mr Thomas Pigeon at a post office about one hundred and twenty miles away, and marked 'to be left 'till called for'.

Whicher then followed the letter and introduced himself to the man in charge of the receiving post office, who allowed him to wait on the premises for three days until an ostler called to collect the letter. The post-

[1] Couper (or more usually cooper): one who tampers illicitly, in this case probably with horses to hide their faults before selling. Magsman: Swindler or confidence trickster.

master took his time finding it, which gave Whicher the chance to make rapid exit from his cosy hiding place and saunter outside to where the man stood with his horse by the open shop window.

'Why, this is Mr Jones's mare,' exclaimed Whicher, patting the animal.

'No. It ain't', replied the ostler.

'No?' said Whicher, 'She's very like Mr Jone's mare!'

'She ain't Mr Jones's mare, anyhow,' the unsuspecting ostler retorted, 'It's Mr So and So's, of the Warwick Arms.'

For the next couple of days, Whicher was in and out of the bar of the Warwick Arms, where the letter sat waiting behind the mirror above the fireplace — his task made more difficult because, owing to a horse fair, he was unable to get lodgings in the pub itself. Eventually, Whicher decided to take the initiative. He addressed a letter to a Mr *John* Pigeon at the Warwick Arms and, next morning, managed to dash over to the inn through the pouring rain — just ahead of the postman, who came in to ask whether a Mr John Pigeon resided there.

'No! — stop a bit though', said the barmaid to the postman; she took the first letter down from behind the glass, looked at it, but found that it said Thomas not John, 'and *he* is not staying here. Would you do me a favour, and post this for me, as it is so wet?' The postman agreed, whereupon she put the letter inside another envelope and addressed it to yet another post office, this time in Northamptonshire. Whicher's next three days were spent inside the Northamptonshire post office until, eventually, a man on horseback arrived to collect the letter. But it was not handed over until he said where he was from — another inn, 'a solitary sort of house, a little in the horse line, about a couple of miles from the station'.

Shortly after Whicher had arrived at the solitary sort of house, he spotted three men sitting by the fire in a side room, 'a sort of parlour, or kitchen' — one of them answering the description of Tally-ho Thompson. He joined them, but the atmosphere became strained and cool, and soon Thompson left. 'It turned out afterwards that he was wanted by a Northampton officer for something else', Whicher told Dickens, 'and that, knowing that officer to be pock-marked (as I am my*self*), he mistook him for me.'

Whicher was still uncertain whether the man was Thompson, but he followed him outside, where he found him talking to the landlady in the yard, and took a chance. 'Tally-ho Thompson, it's no use. I know you', he said, putting a hand on the man's shoulder, 'I'm an officer from London, and I take you into custody for felony!' Thompson swore, and, not surprisingly, the prisoners' friends were none too pleased with the developments either. When Whicher took his prisoner back into the parlour they began harassing him, but Whicher turned on them: that he was not alone there, whatever they might think, he knew them, and they had better watch themselves. 'I'd never seen or heard of them in my life, but my bouncing cowed 'em a bit, and they kept off, while Thompson was making ready to go.'

Thompson's friends were big men, and it occurred to Whicher that they might well follow him up the long, dark, and lonely road to the railway station and attack him. He demanded to be told how many men were employed by the house. The landlady denied there were any, but had to admit to the young ostler. Whicher had him fetched, called upon him in the Queen's name to assist him, and warned him of dire consequences should he decline. 'You never saw a person open his eyes so wide.' The whole situation was clearly on a knife edge, but when the officer took out his handcuffs his prisoner became distraught, begging not to have the shame of being taken in them and promising that, if they were not used, he would come quietly. So, after brandies all round, Whicher, Thompson, and the ostler wended their way unmolested to the railway station.

'He was afterwards acquitted', the sergeant admitted, 'on account of a defect in the evidence; and I understand he always praises me up to the skies, and says I'm one of the best of men.'

'After a little grave smoking', Inspector Field fixed his eye on his host and announced: 'It wasn't a bad plant that of mine, on Fikey, the man accused of forging the Sou'-Western Railway debentures—it was only t'other day—because the reason why? I'll tell you.'

Field knew that Fikey had a carriage factory on the Surrey side of the river, but had been unable to catch him in, so wrote a letter 'in an assumed name', saying he had a bargain horse and shay [chaise] to dispose of and would drive down the next day to show it to him. Field and Shaw then hired 'a precious smart turn-out' from a friend, but when they arrived at Fikey's factory, and saw the number of 'strong fellows' working there, they decided that arrest on the premises was not a good idea.

At first, Fikey proved unavailable but his brother, on being persuaded that the bargain had to be seen then or not at all, eventually fetched him down from the loft to peruse the 'precious smart turn-out', which he admired immediately.

'And there's a horse!'—for I saw him looking at it. 'Rising eight!', I says, rubbing his fore-legs. (Bless you, there ain't a man in the world who knows less of horses than I do, but I'd heard my friend at the Livery Stables say he was eight years old, so I says, as knowing as possible, 'Rising eight.') 'Rising eight, is he?' says he. 'Rising eight,' says I. 'Well,' he says, 'What do you want for it?'

Field mentioned a very reasonable price and offered to take only half in cash and let Fikey 'do a bit of stiff' (give a bill) for the balance. Fikey was attracted, and let himself be persuaded to give the turn-out a try. They drove past a pub where one of the railway clerks had been set up to identify him through the window. But Fikey had shaved off his whiskers and the clerk wasn't sure. Fikey thought it a clever little horse, which trotted well, and that the shay ran light. Field agreed, then pounced.

> 'And now, Mr Fikey, I may as well make it all right, without wasting any more of your time. The fact is, I'm Inspector Wield,[2] and you're my prisoner.'
> 'You don't mean that?' he says.
> 'I do, indeed.'
> 'Then burn my body,' says Fikey, 'if this ain't *too* bad!'

Fikey was all for going back to his factory for his coat; but Field was taking no chances and sent for it, 'and we drove him up to London, comfortable'.

Smith's 'Butcher's Tale' was told and, to round off the evening, the middle-aged and soldierly Sergeant Thornton described his chasing of a Jew called Mesheck, who had been 'carrying on, pretty heavily, in the bill-stealing way'. Thornton followed the trail from Chatham to Cheltenham and then from Birmingham to Liverpool, where Meshek and his carpet-bag, emblazoned with a green parrot, were lost to the detective. A year later, the Jew by then forgotten, Thornton had to cross the Atlantic in search of an Irish bank robber. After capturing him, he lodged the robber in 'a New York prison called the Tombs' — which he dared say Dickens knew? Dickens did. Next day they passed through the New York magistrates' private room, and sitting there was the carpet-bag — green parrot and all.

'That Carpet Bag, with the representation of a green parrot on a stand', Thornton announced to the New York policemen, 'belongs to an English Jew, named Aaron Mesheck, and to no other man, alive or dead!'

'I give you my word', he told Dickens, 'the New York Police Officers were doubled up with surprise.'

---

[2] Dickens 'disguised' the detectives, calling them Wield, Dornton, Witchem, Mith, Fendall, and Straw. Walker he called Stalker.

The Jew was, of course, under arrest for another offence, and in his give-away bag was more evidence regarding the offences he had committed in England.

As the world knows, it was that ebullient character, Field, who was to become the author's favourite policeman. He and Sergeants Thornton and Smith returned to the *Household Words* offices on another summer's evening. This time, Field was ready with an anecdote concerning the tracking down of the ownership of the pair of gloves found at the scene of the murder of Eliza Grimwood, then carried on to relate 'one of the most *beautiful* things that ever was done, perhaps.' This was 'a move of Sergeant Witchem's . . . a lovely idea'.

It seems that, between seeing in the trains at Epsom on Derby Day, Whicher and Field were having a glass of sherry with a friend when four of the swell mob dashed in and snatched the friend's diamond tie-pin. Sergeant Whicher immediately cut them off at the door, and a battle royal ensued. They all ended up at a crowded Epsom police station but Field, finding nothing on their prisoners, was bemoaning of lack of evidence when Whicher opened his hand to reveal the pin. He had seen who had taken it, he told Field, and while they were all scrapping on the floor he had given the man a little touch on the back of his hand, 'as I knew his pal would; and he thought it WAS his pal; and gave it to me!'

The Detective Branch was so well chosen and trained, declared Dickens, proceeded so systematically and quietly, did its business in such a workmanlike manner, and was always

> so calmly and steadily engaged in the service of the public, that the public really do not know enough of it, to know a tithe of its usefulness . . . These games of chess, played with live pieces, are played before small audiences, and are chronicled nowhere. The interest of the game supports the player. Its results are enough for Justice.'

He was to change that state of affairs, greatly surprising the public both by what he revealed about the work of the branch and by the fulsome tone of his approval:

> For ever on the watch, with their wits stretched to the utmost, these officers have, from day to day and year to year, to set themselves against every novelty of trickery and dexterity that the combined imaginations of all the lawless rascals in England can devise, and to keep pace with every such invention that comes out.

Some have scratched their heads over Dickens's fascination with the detective police, but there is nothing surprising about it. They were a passport to another world into which not even he could wander unescorted. It is an interest most people continue to feel today, despite all the anti-police rhetoric. Why else should we have the endless police films and TV series? They are where things happen, and they offer a heady mixture of adventure, danger, power, order, discipline, comradeship, exclusivity, play-acting for real, and getting away with some outrageous behaviour on the grounds of being in the right.

It had not been Dickens himself who first lighted on these fascinating folk in 1850, but his *Household Words* assistant, W. H. Wills, who contributed *The Modern Science of Thief-Taking* to the new journal. In it, he compared what happened when a simple constable came in answer to your message that your house had been robbed (he declared your locks had been 'wiolated' and cast disturbing aspersions on your servants) with the splendid service you received when one of the divisional detectives appeared. After a rapid perusal he would reveal which 'school' of thieves had committed the act and how they had gained entrance over the roof, then go to see which of the appropriate garretters (smelters down of stolen goods) had smoking chimneys or other signs of activity that night, reappearing in the morning with some of your goods.

Wills also painted a beguiling picture of the electrifying effect the appearance of one 'plain, honest-looking fellow, with nothing formidable in his appearance, or dreadful in his countenance' (a detective) has on some seemingly elegant Parisian figures at an out-of-town soirée.

> 'You never saw such a change as his presence causes, when he places his knuckles on the edge of the table and looks at the diners *seriatim*.
> . . . You now, most impressively, understand the meaning of the word 'dumbfoundered'.

The diners are, in fact, 'members of a crack school of swell mobsmen', and the detective is ensuring that they leave forthwith, their bill paid and without any booty. A few quiet words sees a scramble of packing taking place, and, on approaching this powerful person at the railway station, the writer (for he declares 'this is a circumstance that actually occurred') discovers he is 'Sergeant Witchem of the Detective Police'. The fugitives could be clapped inside for 28 days as known rogues and vagabonds, merely on 'Witchem's' say-so and despite not having actually done anything.

It was soon after this piece appeared that Dickens first invited the Detective Branch to his office; and he followed 'A Detective Police Party'

THE REAL THING

(reprinted in *Miscellaneous Papers* as 'The Detective Police') with the 'Three "Detective" Anecdotes' told him by Thornton, Smith, and Field when they visited him again 'one July evening'.

The following year, Field took Dickens on a sightseeing tour of London's sleazier dens of thieves and doss-houses, where the inspector was treated like a sultan. Dickens was to meet Field outside the tall-spired Church of St Giles—in whose grounds rest the remains of many of Tyburn's cull. It was a wet night, but the inspector kept waiting not only Dickens but a detective sergeant, 'weary of speaking French all day to foreigners unpacking at the Great Exhibition', and an assistant commissioner wrapped against weather in an oilskin cloak. As they stood waiting, the damp wind blurred the lines of the street lamps and blew out a pieman's fire. Still no Inspector Field. Eventually a constable appeared, announcing that Mr Field was unavoidably delayed at the new British Museum. He would meet them at St Giles's police station in half an hour.

When, eventually, Field did arrive, the posse—minus the oilskinned assistant commissioner but topped and tailed by uniformed constables carrying lanterns—stepped out into the rookeries of St Giles. It was an area frequently described by Boz and now, again:

> this compound of sickening smells, these heaps of filth, these tumbling houses, with all their vile contents, animate and inanimate, slimily overflowing into the black road . . .

After sampling the dubious delights of Seven Dials they continued by cab, over London Bridge to the Borough—an area now much quieter and more subdued, Dickens found, since the arrival of 'a first-rate man', the 'stern but not unkind'[3] Superintendent Haynes. (Dickens lived in Lant Street in the Borough as a boy—to be near his parents, who were in the Marshalsea debtors' prison there, while he worked in the blacking factory at Hungerford Stairs, on the other side of the river.) What is most surprising about the essay which followed is the relish with which the author relates the not unnatural obsequiousness of the publicans, lodging-house keepers, and their customers towards Inspector Field—a man who probably had the power to have the first two classes of people put out of business and who, without doubt, could have seen the third transported.

On they went, local constables gliding from the shadows at the appointed place to open their cab doors: back over the river to Ratcliff Highway, to

---

[3] Ex-Chief Inspector Timothy Cavanagh, *Scotland Yard Past and Present.*

The scene at a common lodging-house, an illustration by
E. G. Dalziel for Dickens's essay 'On Duty with Inspector
Field'. To the right is one of the uniformed constable
escorts. The piece was first published (unillustrated) in
Dickens's magazine, *Household Words*, in 1850.
(From the Household edition of *Reprinted Pieces*,
Chapman & Hall, 1879)

see 'the houses where the sailors dance', then to Whitechapel, where at last they met some spirited resistance from a lodging-house keeper and distinct sullenness in a kitchen 'crammed full of thieves'. It was, Dickens related later, their most dangerous moment. Through it all, the burly Inspector Field was by turns bluffing, blustering, 'polite and soothing', 'sagacious, vigilant', but, most of all, seeming to know everyone and every place and 'at home wherever we go'—and later to be immortalized as Inspector Bucket in *Bleak House*—fat forefinger and all.

11

THE RISE OF THORNTON
AND WHICHER

THE ILLUSTRATED TIMES was right when, in 1856, it
declared: '"Inspector Field of the Detective Force", as he is generally
called, is not only not an Inspector, but also not a detective, according to
the meaning attached to that word.' The extraordinary fact was that Field,
the man whom Dickens had made the most famous British policeman of
his time, and who even now is the best known of those first detectives,
stayed on in the Detective Branch only a very short time after his glorifica-
tion in *Household Words*. In 1852, the same year as *Bleak House* was published, he left the police to run a private enquiry office.

There he had the conduct (the *Illustrated Times* told its readers) 'of some
of the most remarkable and extraordinary cases that have been brought to
the notice of the public for a series of years'. But it was the most recent, the
poisonings by Dr William Palmer at Rugeley, in Staffordshire, with which
the journal was currently concerned. In the 'Rugeley issue', extensive
coverage was given to the ex-police detective's part in the Palmer investigation, with not only a picture of Field but a lengthy monograph on him,
apparently in recompense for the accusations the journal (and others) had
made against the man. Earlier, it had been alleged that Field had withheld
information gained while investigating the life insurance claims on the
victims — information which could have saved a life.

The Metropolitan Police Detective Branch was not involved in the
Palmer poisonings enquiry, but it had dealt with a sensational case the year
before: the Great Bullion Robbery. This took place on the South Eastern
Railway, and was a rather more sophisticated affair than the more recent
Great Train Robbery. Three large boxes of bullion were bound with iron
straps, sealed, and weighed before being placed in Chubb safes, which
were put into the guard's van of the London–Folkestone express. The
boxes were en route to Boulogne, but when they arrived and were weighed
once more they were found wanting. One box was 40 pounds lighter than it
should have been, while the remaining two were slightly heavier. On

(*Above*) The original 'Scotland Yard', headquarters of the Metropolitan Police (on the left); note the lamp. The building was situated in Great Scotland Yard, behind Whitehall — the Admiralty can be spied through the archway. The Metropolitan Police offices were to spread themselves throughout this yard. Great Scotland Yard itself remains, although the original buildings are all gone — apart from the Clarence public house. New Scotland Yard, completed in 1890, was closer to Parliament Square. In another version of this picture, two top-hatted Peelers take the place of the helmeted bobbies in the foreground. (Courtesy of the Metropolitan Police)

(*Left*) Ex-Inspector Field as featured in the *Illustrated Times* special issue on the Palmer poisonings in 1856.

investigation, it was found that most of the bullion had been removed, to be replaced by sacks of lead shot.

The security had seemed infallible. Each safe had two separate locks, requiring different keys, of which only three sets existed. One was held by the South Eastern's London traffic superintendent, one by the station-master at Folkestone Railway Station, and the third by the captain of the South Eastern Railways Channel ferry. Against none of these gentlemen could a whit of evidence be found. Which was unfortunate for the Metropolitan Police, as they were in need of a triumph, being currently under fire for their handling of the Hyde Park protests against the Sunday Trading Bill that same year. The conviction and transportation of a C Division acting detective officer, Charles King, for imitating Fagin had not helped. For over two years King had been training his child pickpockets to work the very same crowds he had been posted to protect. He was unmasked after his star pupil was caught (while attempting to operate unilaterally), and promptly told all. It was to be a similar lack of honour among thieves which eventually brought about the solving of the Great Bullion Robbery more than a year after it took place.

It transpired that the gold had been removed during the London–Folkestone train journey by four men: Burgess, the train guard; Pierce, a ticket-printer to the company; Tester, a clerk in the South Eastern's London traffic department, and Agar, a professional thief. By means depending on the carelessness of those to whom the keys had been entrusted, the four had been able to obtain wax impressions and thus prepare duplicates. All was revealed when Agar was undergoing penal servitude for another crime. He had left his remaining booty with Pierce, instructing him to take care of his girlfriend, Fanny Kay, and their child. This Pierce failed to do, so Fanny went to the police and blew the whistle, her story being corroborated by a furious Agar, who 'turned approver', giving evidence later against his accomplices.

Police still had to find the culprits. Inspector Thornton and a sprig of a young sergeant, Tanner, chased Tester to Sweden but failed to catch him. However, he soon came home of his own accord and gave himself up. He and Burgess were found guilty of stealing from their employer, and were transported for 14 years. Pierce was convicted of larceny and received two years' imprisonment with hard labour, three months of which were to be spent in solitary confinement.

Foreign travel was about to play an increasing part in the lives of two detective sergeants, Smith and another new man, Frederick Williamson.

THE REAL THING

During the 1830s and 1840s, the unprepossessing figure of Louis Napoleon (Prince Charles Louis Napoleon Bonaparte), grandson of Napoleon I's brother, had become familiar both to London society and to police. One of the more illustrious of the European refugees who thronged the British capital at that time — between attempted revolutions — he was described by an associate as 'the depressed parrot'.

The prince was a selfish, vain, and self-indulgent man, but was also recognised as brave and humane. He had first come to live in London in 1838 at the age of thirty, after being expelled from Switzerland. In March, 1840, Inspector Pearce and Sergeant Otway had thwarted his plans to fight a duel with the man said to be Napoleon Bonaparte's natural son. Later that same year, the prince crossed the Channel to Boulogne with the intention of staging an insurrection, but was captured and imprisoned. Six years later, he escaped and returned to London but, while awaiting the arrival of funds from his Italian estates found himself financially embarrassed. This led him to become involved with a moneylender who defrauded him. The man was charged but acquitted due to a legal technicality. 'The devil must have made such law' was the Prince's comment. Nevertheless, he signed on to become one of the many special constables recruited to cope with the 1848 Chartist procession.

Soon after, Louis Napoleon was back in France where, following the collapse of the government, he managed to get himself elected, first to the National Assembly and then to the presidency. Three years later, the depressed parrot had become Napoleon III, Emperor of France, replacing King Louis Philippe. The new emperor sided with Britain in the Crimean War, exchanged visits with Victoria and Albert, but failed to fulfil promises to help rid Italy of the despotic control of Austria and the papal states and to re-establish their republic which, initially, France had helped to overthrow. Louis Napoleon had intended to right the wrongs — but political expediency intervened.

This failure did not please London's Italian revolutionaries, some of whom began slipping across the Channel to leave an 'infernal machine' on the Emperor's railway route, or to take pot-shots at him in the Champs-Elysées.

At twenty-five minutes to nine, on the evening of 14 January 1858, the assassination attempts became rather more serious. The heavy state coach bearing Napoleon III and his beautiful, sumptuously gowned, but stupid empress, Eugénie, had just arrived at the Opera, flanked by a troop of lancers, when all hell broke loose. Deafening explosions, flashes of light,

(*Above*) Inspector Bucket, a character Dickens is said to have
based on Inspector Field, searching for clues in Lady
Dedlock's boudoir. Illustration by Fred Barnard for
Bleak House (Household edition, Chapman & Hall, 1873).

(*Below*) New Police waiting to take their charges before the
magistrates at Marlborough Street police court in 1858.

billows of smoke, and a showering of glass were followed by a deathly silence before shrieks of pain and screams of terror began to rend the air. Two bombs had been thrown at the carriage. All around lay the dead and dying; lancers, police, members of the crowd—and horses. Inspector Herbert of the Sûreté dashed forward to wrench open the door of the damaged coach—just as a third bomb exploded beneath. He was seriously wounded, but the occupants were unharmed apart from a scratch to the emperor's nose and inflammation to the empress's eye caused by flying glass.

The bombing killed two people outright. Six more died within 48 hours and 156 were injured—some of them quite dreadfully. In all, 516 separate wounds were counted in the victims.

One Italian revolutionary, Giuseppe Pieri, had been spotted and arrested beforehand by Inspector Herbert. The others, Antonio Gomez, Carlo di Rudio, and the ringleader, Felice Orsini, himself wounded, were arrested soon afterwards. Orsini carried a British passport in the name of Thomas Allsop, but when questioned by a French superintendent as to how far he lived from London he answered, 'About thirty kilometres'. This convinced the crafty policeman that he had his man, as a genuine Englishman would have said, 'twenty miles'. Naturally, the trail led back to London. All the plotting had been done there by Orsini and his fellow conspirators. The fiendish fragmenting grenades were manufactured (to order) by a Mr Taylor of Birmingham, and the filling provided by a French communist refugee, Dr Simon Bernard. The whole became a grenade of 'unprecedented power'.

These revelations made Britain, that 'nest of vipers', even less popular than usual across the Channel. As Baron Hübner, the Austrian ambassador to France, noticed, 'France seemed as if drunk with anger and hatred of England'. This may have seemed a little unreasonable to the likes of Sir Richard Mayne,[1] who was to insist that he had kept the Sûreté informed not only of the movements of Orsini and Pieri, but also of their plans.

Two of the three important conspirators not arrested in Paris were English: Chartist Thomas Allsop (Orsini's passport supplier) and a wealthy young man, J. D. P. Hodge. The third was the explosives expert, Dr Simon Bernard. The British government was pressurized into action, and a month after the assassination attempt, French-speaking Sergeant Frederick Adolphus Williamson of the Detective Branch was sent to

[1] Mayne was knighted in 1851.

Bernard's lodgings in Bayswater to arrest him. Williamson was one of the new breed of detective sergeants beginning to surface in the department — more privileged, better educated, and lighter-hearted than their predecessors, possibly for the previous reasons and because they were not obliged to be trail-blazers. Some of them may well have received their coveted positions through influence. For instance, Williamson's father was superintendent of the T Division, and the jolly and popular young Frederick had found his way into the detective branch only two years after joining the Metropolitan Police in 1850.

Sergeant Williamson found Dr Bernard in his dressing gown which, if his outdoor clothes were anything to go by, was probably grubby and egg-stained. Like many refugees, he made his living by teaching languages, but also did work as a speech impediment consultant. Unlike the handsome, bearded Orsini, Dr Bernard, forty-one years old but looking much older, was not cast in the mould of romantic revolutionary. Indeed, he was 'a meagre figure with crumpled shoulders and long arms and legs'.[2] He had long black hair, his complexion was sallow, his forehead receding, his nose large, and his moustache drooped to conceal rabbit teeth. He was also, according to *The Times*, 'below what we in England regard as the middle height', and rather deaf, too, having to cup his ear to catch what people said. However, it was agreed that he had piercing eyes, a brave, simple, and trusting nature, and genuine belief in the justness of his revolutionary causes. Moreover, the whole thing had been his idea.

The thirty-year-old Williamson was not very tall either, but he was handsome, confident, and brimming with life and liberty. He refused to allow Bernard to go upstairs for his clothes, but sent for them, making the doctor dress in the downstairs kitchen, where he read out the warrant. 'If I have done wrong, I must suffer for it' was Bernard's ambiguous response.

In the cab on the way back to Scotland Yard, he asked Williamson why he had not allowed him to go upstairs. Was he afraid? 'I had a right to take precautions for my own sake as well as yours', was the detective's judicious reply — or, at least, the one he quoted at the trial. 'You have no occasion to be afraid', the wispy doctor assured him, 'you are an Englishman, if you had been a Frenchman I would have killed you.' Later, while searching upstairs, the detective may have wondered about the sincerity of that statement. He found a revolver and a knuckle-duster — the latter, he explained to the jury at the trial, was 'an American invention'.

---

[2] Michael St John Packe, *The Bombs of Orsini*.

THE REAL THING

The bilingual Sergeant Williamson and the ex-butcher Sergeant Smith shuttled back and forth across the Channel, gathering evidence and making prosecution arrangements with the French police. Inspector Whicher set off in pursuit of one of the remaining plotters still at large — Thomas Allsop.

Bernard's trial began on a fine but distinctly chilly morning in mid-April 1858. The floor of the Old Bailey was soon awash with French and Belgian witnesses — some blinded or on crutches from their injuries — and the bench alive with persons of note, including the French ambassador and Sir Richard Mayne, while Chartists and foreign refugees thronged the specially enlarged public gallery. French policemen, medical men, a gunsmith, and even a Parisian veterinary surgeon trooped in and out of the witness box. Then came the British police contingent, beginning with Whicher, who said he had not yet found Allsop although he had been searching for five weeks, and followed by Sergeant Rogers, who was something of a revelation to the court. 'Rogers the spy', defence counsel Edwin James was to insist on calling him.

Rogers's exploits were probably the reason why Mayne — doubtless alerted by Bernard's loose tongue and his bomb test at Putney (which caused the neighbours to complain) — had been able to warn the French police. Sergeant Rogers, a man of eight years' service, mostly in uniform, understood French as well as he did English. Since the previous November, he revealed, he had been instructed by Sir Richard Mayne to watch French and Italian refugees. He was particularly called upon to attend their political debates held at Thomas Wyld's reading and debating rooms in Leicester Square — which were part-owned by Bernard. The defence leapt on this witness as typical of the whole affair. Rogers was clearly in the pay of the French government, James insinuated, and the French were trying to bring their spying, tyrannical ways to London. (There had been a purge in France following the bomb outrage, which may have added weight to this dramatic stance.)

Inspector Saunders[3] was another policeman whose name kept popping up. 'The ever-busy and ubiquitous Mr Saunders', James termed him. Much was also made of the part played by Williamson and Smith — in particular how, with Saunders, they had acquired the services of two

[3] According to Alan R. Pike (unpublished MS, *Man from the Yard*), Inspector Saunders had a mistress in Paris who was always well up in the latest gossip from the underworld, so he was much used to follow-up cases in France. Later he was to become an alcoholic and commit suicide.

female witnesses. These were Eliza Rudio and Eliza Cheyney, the 'housekeeper' of Orsini. The policemen not only took them to Paris several times to visit their men before the expected execution, but kept Mrs Rudio closeted in comfort in the Bedford Hotel until the trial. In the event, Rudio was reprieved, but by the time of Bernard's trial Orsini and Pieri had been guillotined.

It was the first time that such a charge relating to a crime committed abroad had taken place in a British court, and defence counsel was to make much of this. He alleged to the all-British jury (Bernard had been offered a 50 per cent alien jury but had declined, saying he trusted the British) that the emperor was attempting to destroy the very asylum of which he himself had taken advantage.

'Tell the French Emperor that he cannot intimidate an English Jury', he implored. 'Tell him that though six hundred thousand French bayonets glittered before you, though the roar of French cannon thundered in your ears you will return a verdict which your own breasts and consciences will sanctify and approve. . . .' It was Waterloo all over again, and, despite a summing up in favour of a guilty verdict, the jury found Dr Simon Bernard not guilty. Their pronouncement, *The Times* reported, brought 'a loud shout of exultation' from the public gallery—echoed by the crowds outside. France, which had spent £30,000 on the case, was furious but, again, expediency soon healed the breach.

A couple of months later another hot potato re-emerged—the unsolved murder of P C Clark—but at least it was not political. Clark's shade had been haunting a Mrs Smith of Dagenham who, when the murder occurred, had been married to William Page, the brother of Ralph Page—whose sons had led the police to the body. William Page had been killed in an accident a year after P C Clark's murder in 1846, and his wife had remarried. But for some time she had been telling neighbours that she knew who the murderers were. It was June again, the corn was high, and (as at the time of the crime twelve years before) the weather was steamy. It was so hot, in fact, claimed *The Times*, that all London was 'sinking under pressure of a Bengal sun'. Mrs Smith now imparted her guilty knowledge to the police; the murderers were her dead husband and three other men: Ned Wood, George Chalk, and George Blewett.

Mayne handed the case to the man who was later referred to by a colleague as 'the prince of detectives', Jonathan Whicher, now promoted to Inspector and, with Thornton, in charge of the Detective Branch. As a sergeant he had been part of the Clark murder investigation team, so was familiar with the inward-looking rural area and the wily characters involved.

Ned Wood, he discovered, had hanged himself some time earlier and Chalk was gone from Dagenham, allegedly to Australia. The only accused man still around was George Blewett. Whicher, armed with a warrant, arrested Blewett as he was working in the fields of a Mr Seagrove. It might have been a smarter move to obtain a little corroborative evidence first; but Whicher, despite the fact that he was to be described as 'quiet, shrewd, and practical, never in a hurry', does, in retrospect, give the impression of being sometimes too quick off the mark. On 28 June 1858 Blewett stood before the Ilford magistrates charged with the crime — twelve years, all but a day, since Clark's murder.

The story which Mrs Smith had to tell sounded feasible, particularly as it had supposedly taken place during 'the hungry forties', and in that lawless area. According to her, on the night of the murder the four men decided to steal corn from the barn of Mr Brettan, a farmer who in fact employed two of them, Page and Blewett. Ralph Page was to be waiting to stow the corn into his barn. They discussed the possibility of being caught by P C Clark and decided that, should he interfere, they would 'serve him out'. Clark *did* appear, whereupon Mrs Page, who had been left outside Mr Brittan's barn as a lookout, called to warn her husband. He came out 'with a loaded stick' and asked the policeman why he was watching them. It was his duty, Clark declared, whereupon William Page set about him with the stick, striking him several severe blows on the upper part of the body, and shouting warnings to his fellow thieves. They came out, armed with pitchforks, and surrounded the hapless officer. Mrs Page fled home.

Later that night she helped her husband burn his bloodstained smockfrock and trousers. After schooling her as to the story she should tell the police — that they had gone to bed at ten o'clock and stayed there all night — Page told his wife they had killed P C Clark and taken his body the quarter mile to the field (where he was later found). There, Chalk had beaten in the P C's skull with the heel of his boot.

On the evening after the body had been found, the Pages and Blewett had gone to Romford and, while on the road, Blewett had said to Page, 'Who would have thought of seeing the policeman there?' Page had replied: 'No, but we well served him out for his trouble.' 'But I never thought it would come to that,' Blewett had added.

Mrs Page had lived with this guilty knowledge ever since, but was frightened of dying with it. What was needed now was corroboration. The arrest, the local superintendent wrote to the commissioners, had caused considerable excitement in the area. Rumours of new evidence abounded, and the superintendent himself enclosed a statement from Thomas Hunnicut, 'the Brentford billsticker', who believed he was the last person to see Clark before the murder when, at midnight, he had bread and cheese with the constable in Mr Seabrook's turnip-mashing shed. He was then acting as Mr Seabrook's watchman and, after arranging to meet Clark later, had gone off to inspect the premises. Clark had not appeared at their proposed second meet. The previous evening, Hunnicut claimed, he had spotted three men in short frocks or coats go down the lane, and a few nights before he had seen some men stealing potatoes from his master's field, although they had fled when he fired his gun. Moreover, at about ten o'clock on the night of the murder, Sergeant Parsons had passed by, on horseback, and had asked him if he had seen any of his men. This was 'very singular' since the sergeant had never spoken to him before.

The helpfulness of this 'evidence' proved to be general. If all the rumours which had been busily circulating were true, Whicher told the magistrates on later hearings, they would have been 'highly important to the case'. But, alas, they were not, and he was unable to produce any more concrete evidence. One witness, he pointed out, who was now declaring that he had seen Clark pass his house late on the night of the murder, had actually 'stated quite the contrary at the inquest'. None the less, it was an important and mysterious case, decided the magistrates, which had had a great deal of publicity and should therefore be submitted to another tribunal. Blewett, despite his protestations of innocence, was sent for trial, and Whicher respectfully suggested to the commissioners that, it being a capital offence and having regard to the length of time which had elapsed, legal aid should be obtained for the prosecution. As well as being aware that he needed all the help he could get, Whicher was being tactful. The bench had already shown surprise that the commissioners had not instructed counsel to attend, while an 'Inhabitant of the Neighbourhood', in a letter to *The Times* had claimed that this was indicative of the lack of zeal with which police would pursue the matter 'unless urged through the Press'.

At Chelmsford assizes Mr Justice Willes, one of Her Majesty's more emotional judges, who tended to weep when sentencing people to death and was later to commit suicide, told the Grand Jury that the evidence was 'of a most peculiar character'. He made it plain that the lack of corroboration was serious — as was the fact which had emerged under cross examination at the police court: that Mrs Smith believed she was haunted by her husband's ghost and appeared to be suffering from hallucinations. She claimed to have seen a fire engine in her room and seen the devil when he came to eat her food. Not surprisingly, the true bill was returned 'not found'.

Later that year the commissioners received a letter from the commissioner of the Melbourne Police, who had read the story in *The Sunday Times*. The letter stated that a man named Henry Chalk resided 'in this Colony' and, about fifteen months earlier, 'was heard to state that he knew the constable who was murdered and that he must have disturbed them taking smuggled tobacco from a farm'. Whicher, when asked for his comments, said that the description of 'about fifty' did not tally with George Chalk's age which would now be about 30 years, and, in any case, that there was insufficient evidence against him.

This, apart from later speculation that Clark may have been having an affair with Parsons's wife, was the last word on PC Clark's murder. One may still see his splendid memoral plinth in old Dagenham churchyard, opposite the still-existing Cross Keys public house where the inquest hearings took place. The inscription reads:

> Sacred to the memory of George Clark, late a Police Constable of the K Division of the Metropolitan Police, who was inhumanely and barbarously murdered in a field at Eastbrook End, in this Parish whilst on duty on the night of the 29th or the morning of the 30th June 1846, aged 20 years.
>
> His uniform good conduct gained him the respect of all who knew him and his melancholy end was universally deplored.
>
> This tribute of respect was erected by the inhabitants of this parish and his brother officers of the K Division of the Metropolitan Police.

12

CRISIS

I AM DIRECTED by the Secretary Sir George Lewis to request that an intelligent officer of the Metropolitan Police be sent down to assist the magistrates in the investigation of the recent murder of Mr Kent's child at Road.

So began a letter to Sir Richard Mayne from the Home Office on 14 July 1860. Mayne sent his prince of detectives, Jonathan Whicher. Only six days after the inspector had left his home at Millbank to take up temporary residence at the Woolpack inn in Trowbridge, Mayne received a message from him, transmitted by the electric telegraph.

I have this day apprehended on warrant Constance Kent the third daughter. She is remanded for a week. The Magistrates have left the case entirely in my hands to get up the evidence. I am awkwardly situated and want assistance. Pray send down Sgt Williamson or Tanner.

He got Williamson and, a couple of days later, wrote a long letter to Mayne explaining just why he was 'awkwardly situated' and the details of the case to date.

On the morning of 29 June 1860, the cot of four-year-old Francis Kent, apple of his mother's eye, had been found empty. Later, the child's body was discovered in the outside privy in the grounds of Road Hill House, the Kents' handsome and spacious residence situated on the outskirts of the isolated village of Road on the Somerset/Wiltshire border. The fact that two local police forces instantly became involved was only one of the many complications of the case.

Their lack of experience in detection also hampered the subsequent investigations — particularly under the intense public scrutiny which this case was to attract. They deduced that the crime must have been committed by a member of the household and, like many households at that time, this was large and complex. At its head was factory inspector Mr

William Kent, an unpopular man locally due to his high-handed ways. The others were his second wife (who was very pregnant) and their three children, all under five; three servants; and four offspring by his first wife. Two of these were adult daughters, the others being William and Constance, who were in their mid-teens.

Under much pressure for results, local police arrested Elizabeth Gough, the nursemaid in whose room the victim slept—there had been some gossip that she was Kent's mistress. But Elizabeth was soon released due to lack of evidence, and at this point Scotland Yard was called in.

Whicher swiftly concentrated on the 15-year-old Constance Kent. He had learned of the suspicion that she had previously attempted to harm her half-brother Francis by stripping off his bedclothes and socks during the night; of her odd reaction on hearing that Francis was missing—she stood close by but said nothing; of her fascination with the trial of the suspected murderess, Madeleine Smith, a few years earlier; and finally, of the insanity on her mother's side of the family. Mr Kent had volunteered the information that Constance's mother, grandmother, and uncle had each been 'of unsound mind' to some degree; while two local doctors, both of whom knew the girl well, confided to Whicher that the girl was 'affected with homicidal tendencies'. One even went so far as to declare that he would not sleep in the same house as her. Added to this mass of suspicion, a schoolfriend revealed that Constance had told her she disliked her half-brother, and that she was not looking forward to returning home for the summer holidays. On finding that one of Constance's nightdresses had been 'lost' in the wash (after the girl had engineered being left alone with the laundry basket), he reported back to the magistrates—who issued a warrant for Constance Kent's arrest

which they desired me to execute having previously sworn me as a constable for the county of Wilts. I pointed out to them the unpleasant position such a course would place me in with the County Police especially as they hold opinions opposed to mine . . . [they still strongly suspected Mr Kent and Elizabeth Gough] but the magistrates declined to alter their determination stating that they considered and wished the inquiries to be entirely in my hands, and these circumstances induced me to telegraph for assistance. . . . I am still pursuing my inquiries assisted by Sgt Williamson for whose presence I beg respectfully to thank Sir Richard Mayne as I am very unpleasantly situated as regards acting with the County Police in consequence of the natural jealousy entertained in this matter by them as our opinions

differ . . . and should it appear in the end that my opinions are correct
they would be considered at fault but I have studiously endeavoured to
act in concert with them as far as possible.

The man from Scotland Yard was on a hiding to nothing and he knew it.
The antagonism his antennae were picking up was to prove overwhelm-
ingly strong. His protestations about endeavouring to 'act in concert' may
well have been as a result of his early history in this respect when, shortly
after the department was launched, he was one of the two sergeants (the
other was Smith) reprimanded by Mayne for showing 'want of respect' to
senior, uniformed officers.

For the police court hearing, Constance Kent had the benefit of clever
counsel, a Mr Edlin brought down from Bristol. The prosecution was not
represented, a fact which the inspector felt keenly and later pointed out to
the commissioners. Unopposed, Mr Edlin ran rings around the J Ps, the
clerk, and (inevitably) Inspector Whicher. He almost took control of the
proceedings, and whipped up sympathy for 'this young lady' to such an
extent that the public gallery frequently erupted into bursts of supportive
applause.

Whicher had no *real* evidence, the smooth-tongued lawyer insisted; his
anxiety to arrest someone and claim the reward showed ineffable meanness
and was a disgrace and discredit to the police, particularly in the way he
had hunted up Constance's schoolfriends to give flimsy evidence. The
magistrates had already ruined the girl's life, they ought now at least to give
her freedom. They did — releasing her in her father's bond of £200 — and
she was discharged. The crowd cheered Constance as she left court
(vindicated, as they saw it, though in truth the case against her was merely
considered insufficient to commit for trial and the door had thus been left
open) and shouted insults at the beleaguered Whicher. Soon, most of the
Press joined in the abuse of the Scotland Yard detective, in a manner
typified by an entry in *The Annual Register* for that year:

> The grounds on which this accusation were made were so frivolous
> and the evidence by which it was attempted to be supported so chil-
> dish, that the proceedings can only be described as absurd and cruel.

If anyone was guilty of ineffable meanness, the author Bernard Taylor
points out in his book, *Cruelly Murdered*, it was Edlin, who not only
destroyed an honest and hard-working policeman that day but also exposed
a simple washerwoman to similar hateful insults by accusing her of stealing
the missing nightdress.

Whicher returned to London, after assuring the Trowbridge magistrates that he had no hope of finding further evidence against Constance and that he suspected no one else, with the exception of her brother William, who could possibly have been her accomplice. As the storm broke about his head the magistrates, supported by *The Times* and the *Journal*, attempted to back him up. The local police, delighted at his discomfiture, none the less tried to find the nightdress, the disappearance of which in the first place had been largely due to their negligence at the scene. Eventually, they returned to Mr Kent and Elizabeth Gough, re-arrested her in the hope she would tell all, but, again, had to release her for lack of evidence.

Meanwhile, the Stepney murder was now in the news, and the Press and public began linking the police performance in this case, with that in the Road murder. This time, Thornton was in charge of the enquiry. The drama had begun when a Mr Rose, solicitor to the 70-year-old, wealthy widow Mrs Mary Emsley, went to the police to report that his client appeared to be missing. One of her tenants, Walter Emms, a shoemaker who occasionally collected some of the rents from her considerable property and did odd jobs for her, had gone to see her on Wednesday, 15, Thursday, 16, and Friday, 17 August 1860, but had received no reply to his repeated knockings.

Sergeant Dillon, of the K Division, accompanied Mr Rose and a relative of Mrs Emsley to 9 Grove Road, Bethnal Green, where they let themselves in through the garden door at the back and entered the seemingly undisturbed house. It was a different story in the upstairs front room where Mrs Emsley liked to sit by the window. Her body lay in a sea of congealed blood, surrounded by rolls and fragments of wallpaper. The repeated blows she had suffered to the skull were so severe that they had driven pieces of bone right through her brain.

In answer to divisional requests for detective assistance Thornton sent the lively, 28-year-old Sergeant Richard Tanner and Sergeant William Thomas, an ex-grocer from Bagshot. They discovered that Edward Jackson, a soldier and a nephew of Mrs Emsley, was a bad character and frequently wrote home enquiring whether the old girl was dead yet as he expected to inherit something. Should Tanner be sent down to Portsmouth to see whether Jackson had been absent from his barracks at the time of the murder or should the enquiry be sent by telegraph? Thornton now asked an assistant commissioner. 'Telegraph inquiry to the Police—and if the soldier has been absent, P S Tanner may be sent at once', was the reply. Edwards had not been absent, and this was the start of another case in which there were a seemingly limitless number of suspects and little hard evidence. '. . . there is nothing stolen which can be traced beyond a ten pounds cheque which has been stopped', Thornton reported, 'but I am of the opinion that the murderer will not make use of that, no weapon was left behind, no person was seen near the house on the evening in question.' Not only that, some of Mrs Emsley's tenants were 'of the most depraved and lowest class', he went on. 'She was in the habit of personally collecting the greater portion of her rents on a Monday and in consequence of her frequent litigation with her tenants, her very plain way of dressing and living, she became well-known at the East End of London.'

Indeed, her solicitor had warned her she would be murdered if she continued to go about alone among such bad and dangerous characters. Moreover, Thornton confided, she had let her many poor relatives know that she intended to leave her money to build almshouses. Suspects galore.

The explanation for the wallpaper around the body was that the widow, ever eager for a bargain, had bought a job-lot at a local auction. Thornton assumed, probably quite rightly, that someone had called on her that fateful evening on the pretence of buying some. The only problem with that assumption was that the old lady was very careful who she let into the house. Only those known to her were allowed across the threshold — people such as Walter Emms and an ex-K Division police sergeant, James Mullins, an Irishman who did plastering and papering for her — but the K Division plain-clothes officers who tailed them came up with nothing. In any case, the trail was cold even before they had found the body.

Thus the Stepney murder joined the Road murder as a stick with which to beat the detective police for their lack of results. By 8 September *The Times* was reporting that the police efforts to catch the murderer of Mrs Emsley appeared fruitless: 'at times they are ready to abandon the investigation as hopeless.' The very next day, Thornton and Tanner made two arrests for the murder — arrests which had come about by a most curious set of circumstances.

Ex-policeman Mullins had called on Sergeant Tanner at his home in Stepney, saying that he had some information to offer. He had been to Thornton's house but he was not in. He said that since 28 August, when Tanner had interviewed him as a suspect, he had been studying the case, using his police experience, and had developed suspicions about the shoemaker, Emms. He had begun following him that very morning (8 September) at five o'clock by going to the field in which Emms's cottage stood — on the pretext of collecting herbs.

147

While there, his quarry had emerged from the cottage, walked to a ruin nearby, and come out carrying a large parcel. This he had taken into his premises, only to re-emerge ten minutes later carrying a smaller parcel, which he then placed in the adjacent shed. Tanner refused to take any action on this information without telling Thornton first, but promised to keep Mullins apprised of its use. Before taking his leave, Mullins assured Tanner, 'If this goes all right I'll take care of you', meaning of course that he would give Mullins a share of the reward, which had now risen from £100 to £300.

The following morning, a Sunday, Inspector Thornton, Sergeants Tanner and Thomas, and their informant, James Mullins, went by hackney cab to Emms's cottage. They told Mullins to keep in the background while they searched the cottage and outhouse but they found nothing — which may have been deliberate. On hearing this, Mullins exclaimed, 'You have not half searched this place! Come on, I'll show you!' This he promptly did, urging, 'Look there, now, pull down that bloody slab.' Sergeant Thomas did so and (surprise, surprise) found a parcel containing some spoons and the missing cheque. Walter Emms was arrested but, of course, so was Mullins. The shoemaker, having an alibi and no apparent knowledge of the parcel, was released, but the 58-year-old Mullins was charged and sent for trial. In fact, he had already served a six-year sentence for larceny — which had cost him his police pension.

But some of the Press were still not pleased. The police had done it again, complained the *Illustrated Times* — arrested someone before they had sufficient evidence. It was time the whole lamentably defective system was looked at, particularly the means of preserving inanimate objects. One only had to look at the evidence about Mrs Emsley's injuries, which relied solely on the recollections of one man (a Doctor Gill), when 'the mute evidence of the wounds might have been perpetuated for centuries by the simple means of a bag of plaster' (footprints had been preserved with plaster since the days of the Bow Street Runners.)

> The position of the body and its surroundings might have been in like manner kept in proof by the aid of the photographer. Yet when — in England, at least — have these simple, yet incontestable, methods of preserving evidence been resorted to in cases of mysterious murder?

Not only that, days or weeks were allowed to pass before a reward was offered.

> This is the very root of evil! We actually employ, at the public charge,
> a body of low, cunning men called 'detectives' and we hold out induce-
> ments of small fortunes to them *not to do their work.*

—that is, there was no profit for the detectives in catching the suspects
quickly.

> Let him allow the matter to become a wonder and a 'mystery', as it is
> termed, and let him then go to work, and if he succeeds it is to his own
> enormous profit, while if he fails it all goes into his day's work.

The detectives did their best to consolidate their case against James
Mullins with many witnesses and an array of forensic evidence. They even
went so far as to cut up a section of Mrs Emsley's floorboards and take
them into court.

On Mullins's mantelpiece Tanner had found a piece of tape similar to
that used to tie the parcel to which he had led them. No, the sergeant
admitted to the trial judge, Chief Baron Pollock, he did not know whether
both pieces had been examined to see whether they had the same number
of threads, but the ends corresponded exactly with each other. Dr Gill was
recalled to state that he had examined the two pieces and found not only
that the ends corresponded exactly but that there were 83 strands in each
piece. No, he was not engaged in the manufacture of tape, but (he told
defence counsel Mr J Best) he was in the habit of examining fabrics in
which he took an interest under the microscope. He had examined a great
many different fabrics in this way—for his own gratification.

A partial imprint of a nailed boot had been found in the blood at the
scene of the crime. Thornton had had that part of the floorboard cut out
and brought to court so that the jury could compare the print with a boot
which Mullins had been seen to throw away. The jury enquired whether
they might have a pair of compasses with which to compare the measure-
ments of the boot and print, but Judge Baron Pollock felt that if it had come
to that the evidence would not carry much weight. Casts of footmarks were
often brought into court but that was not a matter of measurement—they
had to fit the shoe like a seal.

Dr Gill was recalled yet again, and gave evidence that he had examined
the boot with his microscope and found three human hairs which corresponded to those of Mrs Emsley. Yes, he admitted, he realized that human
hair was used by plasterers (in their mortar). He had also examined the
silver pencil case which was believed to be the property of the deceased and
which Mullins had sold after the crime. There was blood on it, he insisted,

the microscope being an infallible aid in proving the presence of blood. Well, no, he couldn't actually say whether the blood was human, there was no test for discriminating that yet.

In addition to Dr Gill and his microscope, police had spoons found on Mullins's premises which were identical with those in the parcel, though of a common type. They also had witnesses who swore to having seen Mullins in the neighbourhood of Grove Road on the night in question. They had been taken to either the house of detention or the police court to pick Mullins out. (According to *The Times*, he looked 'hardly so old' as his 58 years, 'though he wears spectacles', and was 'intelligent and rather pre-possessing' in appearance.)

Identification evidence was notoriously unreliable, the judge told the jury in his summing up, and he also made it clear he did not set much store by the forensic evidence either. The tape was too common to make such assumptions about it and, in any case, he himself could tell that one piece was thicker than the other. The hammer produced as the weapon was a tool common to plasterers and it had not been fair to exhibit it in court. As for the boot, before such evidence was submitted it should be clear to every observer that such a similarity existed between it and the footprint that one must necessarily be the copy of the other — such was not the case.

It may have been pertinent that Baron Pollock was, at that time, in some embarrassment due to a case in which he had summed up *against* the accused — a Dr Smethurst, on trial for allegedly poisoning his mistress — largely on the grounds of 'expert' medical evidence. This had proved to be flawed, and was also well countered by the evidence of experts called by the defence counsel, Serjeant Parry. Smethurst had been found guilty, but such doubts were raised that the Home Office was currently holding an enquiry into the case which was later to result in the accused being set free. *Prosecuting* counsel in the case against Mullins was the same Serjeant Parry.

What the whole case against Mullins rested on, said the judge, was whether they believed Emms or Mullins. They must ask themselves what possible motive Emms could have for secreting the parcel at dawn, as Mullins described, and why he would not have burned such damning evidence as the uncashed cheque.

The jury believed Walter Emms and found James Mullins guilty of murder. But, even when passing sentence of death, Baron Pollock could not resist a smack at Serjeant Parry and the police. When assuring Mullins he thought the jury had come to the right decision, he added, 'I am still of the opinion that some of the circumstances urged against you, instead of increasing the weight of evidence for the prosecution, only tended to embarrass the jury in coming to a conclusion.'

It must have seemed to the Detective Branch that they were damned if they did and damned if they didn't.

13

FOREIGNERS AGAIN

ONE OF THE ODDEST CASES handled by the first detectives was that concerning Baron de Vidil and his son, Alfred. A friend of the Orleans dynasty and said to be the last baron created by King Louis Philippe, de Vidil regularly visited the ex-king and queen at Claremont, a magnificent mansion near Esher in Surrey. Louis Philippe died in 1850, but the baron continued to visit the ex-queen. On a June morning in 1861, he invited Alfred, his 23-year-old son, to accompany him on one of these outings, as had been his custom on previous occasions.

The pair took a train to Twickenham, where ready-saddled horses were waiting to carry them on the long ride down to Claremont. They had recrossed the river on their return journey, tired and hungry, as Alfred had not wanted to stop and dine, when the middle-aged baron suddenly announced that he would ask at an inn on the corner which would be the best route. 'Which astonished me', Alfred later told police, 'as I know the road perfectly well.' The baron took a side-road anyway, without consulting the publican, explaining to his son that he was suffering from a bowel complaint. Alfred asked him why he did not turn back and go to the inn. The baron did turn back — but only after seeing a woman appear at the end of the lane in which they were. He then declined to enter the inn, as it did not seem 'a very nice place'.

At this point, the baron decided they should call upon the Duc D'Aumales, a son of Louise Philippe's, who lived at Orleans House[1] on one of the side-roads running down to the Thames. But he kept leading off down the wrong lanes, and (Alfred later claimed) when he finally reached the right one, he rode straight past the duke's house. Alfred commented on this at the time, but he was a somewhat ineffectual young man, and his father was much bigger and stronger, both physically and mentally. The lane they were now on began curving back towards the main road. They

[1] There was a regular nest of French ex-royals in the area. The Comte de Paris, another of the princes, lived at York House, and the Duc de Nemours was at Bushey Park.

had just passed a particularly shady part when the baron declared, 'We have made a mistake, and must turn back.' By now, not surprisingly, the 'exceedingly delicate looking'[2] young Alfred was becoming more than a little confused. 'I got a little ahead of the Baron', he later explained, 'he being on the right, when I felt a violent blow on my head. I turned round, being all right on the saddle and saw the Baron's hand uplifted with something in it. With this he struck me another blow and again raised his arm. . . .'

What the baron held in his hand was a riding whip which had a heavy, silver-knobbed handle, and it was with this end that he was hitting his son. Young Alfred, a dedicated hypochondriac, now had real reason to fear for his health. He spurred his horse and galloped on until he came upon an old lady and a man chatting by a gate. Springing off, he ran towards them, then fell at their feet, clutching at the old lady's skirt and begging for their protection. A riderless horse careered past followed by a panting baron on foot who, seeing the frozen tableau, took off into the shrubbery. But he soon returned to brazen it out, posing as the concerned father trying to help bathe his boy's bloody head and claiming it was the result of an accident with his horse. A surgeon was called to the Swan inn where Alfred had been taken. He doubted the father's story, believed the son, and instructed his assistant to accompany the pair back to London. The following morning, the Baron de Vidil decided that this was a good moment to take a trip to Paris. He was later arrested and returned into the hands of Sergeant Williamson at Scotland Yard, where he was charged with the attempted murder of his son.

The Detective Branch soon found they had prosecution problems on their hands. Alfred, having given a full and damning statement against his father, now refused to give evidence against him. Inspector Thornton, however, had an ace up his sleeve in the form of a witness to the assault — a young labourer named John Rivers who, on his way to work by the riverside near the Duc d'Aumales' estate, had actually seen the offence committed. The problem now, Thornton informed Mr Corrie, the Bow Street magistrate, was that not only was Rivers seriously ill, he was on the point of death; he would not be able to attend court, and in all probability would not survive until the next hearing.

Corrie duly packed everyone off by train to Twickenham: Baron de Vidil, Alfred and Mr Parker, his protector – uncle, the chief clerk, prosecution

2 *The Times*, 24 August 1864.

and defence solicitors and counsel, Inspector Thornton, and Sergeants Williamson and Smith. They arrived at the police station at about 5.30 p.m. 'by which time', the *Windsor and Eton Express* advised its readers, 'the villagers began to assemble in large numbers'. But the local magistrate, deemed necessary to oversee the proceedings, had not put in an appearance. There was panic for a while as messengers were sent hither and thither until, eventually, a Colonel Bonnethorne rode up, later to be joined by another magistrate, Captain Murray.

The party set off for 'two little tenements called Zion cottages where lay poor John Rivers, a young labouring man in the last stage of decline'. It was to be a strange identification, the baron being placed among the crowd outside the sick man's 'small but very clean' upstairs bedroom, the windows of which were thrown open so that the dying man could pick the baron out. He did so, then went on to give a statement in his now-crowded bedroom which tallied more or less with what Alfred had originally said — apart from Rivers's seeing only the first blow striking the young man. The second, he thought, had hit the horse on the nose.

Back at Bow Street, Alfred persisted in refusing to testify. He was not well, he told Mr Corrie, and did not think he should be pressed to give evidence, as he hadn't thought his complaint would come to this. Mr Corrie thought he should be pressed, and sentenced him to seven days in prison, with the threat that he would send him back until he did do his duty towards his sovereign and society generally. But Corrie later withdrew the sentence when the defence brought in a doctor to swear that such a course would have a serious effect on Alfred's health.

'Inspector Thornton intimated that the Commissioners of Police would proceed with it notwithstanding', reported the *Windsor and Eton Express*, But Mr Corrie thought this a dangerous precedent, and said he must first consult the Home Secretary. They did proceed, and the baron, as had his fellow countryman Dr Bernard, opted for an all-British jury.

The motive appears obvious. On the death of his wealthy English wife the baron had inherited a life interest in £20,000, but had sold this soon after for £4,000 and was now financially embarrassed. Alfred, on the other hand, had received actual capital of £20,000 when he came of age, and had later inherited a further £10,000. If he died intestate, this money would go to his father. Defence argued that the incident was merely the result of a quarrel between father and son (although Alfred said if his father persisted in some of these accusations he would be forced to speak). In any case, they claimed, the prosecution had failed to establish the absence of a will (if there was one, the baron could not inherit) — neither had police produced the whip.

Before the trial really got under way Alfred was brought to the witness stand where, once again, in a 'weak and tremulous' voice,[3] he declined to give evidence for the prosecution. He was promptly put in prison for a month, Mr Justice Blackburn explaining that Her Majesty's judges often found themselves obliged to insist that the poorer classes gave evidence against their relatives.

The baron's faith in the all-British jury was to some extent vindicated. They found him not guilty of attempted murder or grievous bodily harm but guilty of unlawful wounding. Mr Justice Blackburn was almost apologetic. He was sorry to pass such a sentence on a person in his position in life as it would probably fall more heavily on him than another, he said — before he informed the baron he must serve 12 months' hard labour.

Certainly, by all accounts the father and son were an odd couple. A character witness for the defence admitted that the baron was 'of a hasty disposition' (although this may have been meant to show his actions were not premeditated), and the newspapers claimed that his mind was 'affected'. At the same time the baron's counsel had tried to prove that the boy had once been 'confined as a lunatic', although the good uncle claimed he was merely drunk on that occasion.

Alfred served his month and emerged looking pale and ill, but the *Windsor and Eton Express* assured its readers with some glee: 'The Baron, still an inmate of the House of Correction, is employed daily in picking oakum.'

MEANWHILE, not far to the east, the department were involved in yet another complicated case involving foreigners — this time much poorer ones.

The first Metropolitan Police officer to get wind of the occurrence was PC King, who lived at the hitherto tranquil Kingswood, about three miles north of Reigate. Just after 9 a.m. on Tuesday, 11 June 1861 he learned that Martha Halliday, wife of the parish clerk, had been found murdered in a bedroom at Kingswood rectory where, in the vicar's absence, she had been acting as caretaker. Mrs Halliday's hands and feet had been tied with rope, her mouth gagged with a handkerchief and she had suffered a severe

---

[3] *The Times*, 24 August 1861.

blow to the face and head—probably from a bludgeon which had been left nearby.

Although a Metropolitan Police officer was first on the scene, the crime had in fact taken place just 30 yards outside that force's area—and so within the jurisdiction of the Surrey constabulary. As well as calling in a surgeon, P C King sensibly sent messages both to Inspector Fraser at his nearest Metropolitan police station at Banstead, and to Superintendent Coward of the Surrey constabulary at Reigate. Inspector Fraser was taking part in mounted drill at Mitcham, and by the time he reached the murder scene Superintendent Coward was already there, accompanied by the incumbent, the Reverend Taylor. Coward assured the inspector that the bedroom and the rest of the house had been thoroughly searched. So far, nothing of value had been found to be missing. As Inspector Fraser was later to explain to his superintendent, after 'the above intimation' and being outside his area, he did not feel he could institute a further search.

Mayne's communication system seems to have broken down again, for when Mr Alcock, the local MP and the person with whom Mrs Halliday had been in service, arrived at Scotland Yard that evening to impart some information, it was the first the Yard had heard of it. They were not pleased. 'I have sent it to be circulated as early as possible—the Detectives have all left the office', reported Inspector Searle, a newcomer to the Executive Branch. 'One of the Detective Force to immediately assist with the enquiry', Sir Richard Mayne scribbled on the message. Another note, signed by Sergeant Smith, announces, 'Sgt Robinson gone as directed.'

Mayne had no need to be embarrassed. The vigilance of one of his men ensured there were early suspects for the crime. At 2.30 a.m. on the night of the murder, P C Peck, on duty at Sutton, about six miles north of Kingswood, had seen two young men hurrying towards London. They were conversing in a foreign language and had tried to avoid his eye, but he stopped and searched them none the less. The taller of the two, he noticed, seemed depressed and 'hung his head down, and said but little'. The other told him, in a strong foreign accent, that they had come from Cuckfield in Sussex, were very tired, and had no money. They asked him the quickest way to Pye Street in Westminister (a further 12 miles). Finding nothing suspicious on them, P C Peck let them go. It transpired that two young foreigners of a similar description, like 'sailors on the tramp', had been seen about Kingswood on the day before the body was found. Inspector Fraser and P C Peck took themselves off to Westminster to see if they could track them down. They had no luck, but did discover that a man answering the description of one of the suspects had enlisted in the Marines at Westminster. The policemen waited for him to put in an appearance at 10 p.m., as he had been ordered to, but he failed to arrive.

The following day, A Division's Inspector Humphries found another possible suspect — a tramp, 'supposed to be a returned transport' but who claimed to be a whitesmith[4] — from Great Peter Street lodging-house who, upon being arrested for assault on police, had uttered some foreign words. The commissioner instructed that PC Peck go to view this man, but warned that 'care should be taken that he is placed with several others when seen'. He was, and was not identified.

Some inter-force difficulties soon began to emerge, as evidenced by a report from Superintendent Payne of P Division, sent three days after the murder: 'I beg to report that on the body of the murdered woman being removed yesterday for a post mortem examination, a book was found, supposed dropped by the murderers. The book was taken from P C196P King, who found it, by Supt Coward, of the Surrey Constabulary.' The 'book' contained a passport in the name of Johann Carl Franz, birth and baptism certificates in the same name, an unaddressed, begging letter signed 'Krohn', and a letter signed by a celebrated soprano, Madam Teresa Tietjens, who was known for her kindness to distressed fellow Germans. Sergeant Williamson went to see the opera singer at her delightful residence in St John's Wood. She told him how, on the previous Friday, a young German of about 19 years of age, giving the name of Gottlieb, had come to her pleading poverty and asking for her assistance to get back to Hamburg. She had given him a letter addressed to Mr Kroll, the proprietor of the Hamburg Hotel, America Square, in the Minories. Williamson interviewed Mr Kroll, but he had neither seen the young man nor received the letter.

On the day that Williamson reported back, further information was trickling through from the Surrey constabulary regarding two foreigners who had been seen in Reigate on the Sunday before the murder. The description of one of them tallied to a reasonable extent with that of 'Gottlieb' — give or take a year and an inch or two. Both men were fair, whiskerless, and wearing a blue and white striped shirt, although Gottlieb wore a brown coat while the other was recorded as black. Moreover, the young men had, before leaving Reigate on the afternoon before the crime,

---

[4] A worker in tinned or white iron, a tinsmith.

bought a twopenny ball of stout string of the type used to tie the unfortunate Mrs Halliday.

While Sergeant Robinson was down at Kingswood, Williamson was doing most of the legwork in town — calling at steamship companies and St Katherine's Dock to see whether anyone answering Franz's description had left for Hamburg recently. He also made enquiries at the Austrian, Prussian, and Hanseatic embassies and consulates as to whether anyone by the name or resembling the description of Franz had applied for a replacement passport.

Soon, the detective branch was being offered a bevy of young foreign suspects, among them Alfred Despres, a Soho tailor; Richard Hinder, a destitute young Saxon who was picked up, exhausted, in Ratcliffe workhouse having walked from London to Dover and back looking for work; and Auguste Saltzmann, a prisoner in Newgate, arrested by the City Police for having been found in a house for an unlawful purpose.

Despres's employer told police that on the evening of the murder the young man had accompanied him to the National Gallery and the British Museum, and his landlady swore to his presence for the rest of the night. Richard Hinder had worked for a sugar manufacturer in Bristol and a stick-maker in Plymouth before coming to London the previous month but, Whicher admitted, had no friends in the capital to vouch for him. 'Altho' he somewhat answers the description of one of the men concerned in the murder, I do not think he is one of them', he concluded, with his customary certainty. PC Peck subsequently failed to pick out Hinder as one of the men he had stopped on the road at 2.30 a.m. that night.

Auguste Saltzmann, the prisoner in Newgate, was another story. PC Peck failed to pick him out, as did three other witnesses from Reigate and Kingswood, but this did not prevent Whicher (who has been portrayed as half the man he once was since the Constance Kent affair) from stating that, none the less, he had no doubt that Saltzmann was in fact Franz and asking the commissioner's permission for more witnesses to be brought up from Surrey. 'Apprvd.', wrote Mayne in the margin, in his familiar but increasingly hard-to-read scrawl, and signed with the usual cryptic 'R.M.'. Mrs Pether, the woman who sold the men the ball of string, thought she recognized Saltzmann but could not be sure, 'but Susannah Elsey, servant to Mrs Pether, who was present when the string was purchased identifies him from among about a dozen others', Whicher reported. And so did James Bashford, Reigate grocer and parish constable, who had seen the foreigners when he went for a drink in the Cricketers' Arms where they were staying—a fact also gleefully underlined by Whicher.

Still vehemently denying he was Franz—there were so many Germans about, why should the book be his?—Saltzman was arrested and charged with the murder. Inspector Whicher informed the bench that Sir Richard had caused photographic copies of various entries in the book to be taken and sent with facsimiles of various documents to Dresden and other places, so as to prove they belonged to the prisoner. The response, still necessarily via the Foreign Office, was a long time in coming. The Home Office tried to speed things up at one point by writing direct to the British embassy in Dresden who, when they replied, managed to include some details which they had already sent back through the leisurely diplomatic channels. When the Dresden police report finally did arrive, it was a masterpiece of teutonic thoroughness; but by this time Auguste Saltzmann had admitted to being Johann Carl Franz, while claiming that his papers had been stolen.

Franz was born at Konigstein in 1835, Herr Berndt, Dresden's secretary of police, informed his London counterparts. 'He is 68 inches tall, of middle stature, healthy complexion, fair hair and eyebrows, oval chin, desterte[5] teeth, he belongs to the Lutheran church, he is acquainted only with the German language and has no beard. He has no distinguishing marks.' Interestingly, he was the son of Carl *Gottlieb* Franz, an employee of the Saxon and Bohemian Railway. Franz the younger, it transpired, had several children and had worked variously as a shoemaker, labourer, railway attendant, lighterman, and wood raftsman on the Elbe. 'He has no property and is considered a lazy and frivolous person', Berndt confided. In fact, he had served two years in prison for theft. 'He intended to go by Hamburg to England, thence to America and was to have sent money from there to enable his family to join him next spring.'

As well as minute details of the clothes and property Franz carried—down to a crack in the face of his watch—the Dresden police gave an estimate of how much money Franz was liable to have had on arrival here—none. His last wage before leaving had been five thaler, and the fare from Hamburg to Hull was that same amount.[6] 'It is worthy of reflection', Dresden's secretary of police pointed out, .'whether to obtain means, he

---

[5] I have not been able to discover the meaning of this word. It may be an error in the transcription of unfamiliar handwriting.

[6] Later it came to light that in fact he had worked his passage. He had intended to go straight across to Liverpool on arrival and embark for America straight away, but because of bad weather the ship arrived at Hull too late. He tramped across to Manchester with two others, where they applied for assistance to the Society for the Relief of Foreigners.

may not have sold his documents to some rogue who has turned them to an improper account.' (It would be interesting to have heard Whicher's reaction to that piece of intelligence — which, in fact, proved to be an omen.) The documents sent in facsimile were genuine, Scotland Yard was assured. 'A likeness of Franz although known to exist I was not able to trace notwithstanding the great trouble I took', Berndt concluded, adding that there were, however, plenty of people who could identify Franz.

Whicher, who appears to have been increasingly in charge of the investigation, was inundated with further sightings and information with regard to the suspected accomplice. One superintendent at Neath enclosed a photograph of a man who answered the description published in the *Police Gazette*, but all proved fruitless. Reigate magistrates, however, were pleased with the manner in which the Metropolitan Police had handled their side, and particularly with Sergeant Robinson's work. They wrote in this vein to the commissioner when their duties regarding the case had come to an end with Franz being committed for trial.

Whicher had a nail-biting time regarding a witness named Streit who was taking his time appearing in London. He had better leave Saxony *'as soon as possible'*, the Inspector warned, 'as Croydon Assizes commence *on Friday next'*. Streit changed his mind at the last minute, and a substitute named Kielig was drafted in. 'The trial commences tomorrow morning at 10 o'clock', Whicher remarked when advising Sir Richard of the man's nick-of-time arrival. In those days, as we have seen, trials could be over in a day.

The Inspector had built up an impressive chain of evidence linking the various pieces of string and the shirt. When Franz arrived at Wentworth Street lodging-house in Whitechapel,[7] he had given the caretaker a bundle to look after. It contained the shirt 'which answered in every particular the description of that worn by one of the foreigners seen at Reigate and Kingswood', and which was tied with a long piece of new cord 'exactly similar' both to that sold to the pair in Reigate on the day of the murder and to that which had bound the hands and feet of the victim.

He brought to the police court one Robert Cramp, a wholesale cord dealer of Whitechapel, who had sold the cord to Mrs Pether. Cramp declared that it was of an uncommon description; he did not believe another ball could be found within 50 miles. Whicher also brought the twine manufacturer, who swore the string was of his make and, further-

---

[7] Where Dickens had his most dangerous moment.

more, that all the pieces were from the same ball. 'I can say this,' he explained, 'because I hackled the hemp in the rough state and spun it and manufactured it afterwards.' He also wound it into balls. Franz, who continued to deny ever having been near Reigate, claimed he had picked up the piece of string in a tobacco shop in Wentworth Street which (unfortunately for the police case) was, like the cord dealer, in Whitechapel.

Madame Tietjens failed positively to identify the accused, possibly through soft-heartedness; but the biggest blow to the case may have been the finding of a second pocket-book containing more papers in the name of Franz. Whicher's heart must have sunk when these arrived a couple of weeks before the trial. Franz had claimed he was robbed of his papers by a fellow German after sleeping with him and another in a haystack near the Northamptonshire border when on their way south.

Now, a man had presented a second pocket-book to the Banbury magistrates, saying he had found it in some straw in a wood outside the town. Among the papers was a part of a diary about a trip up the Elbe and to Hull, a birth certificate, and a good-conduct certificate issued by the Saxon and Bohemian Railway, both in the name of Franz.

The man who handed these in, William Potts J P told the London police in answer to an urgent telegram, was 'most unmistakably an Englishman'. Of course, there are several explanations for the find, apart from the possibility that it was genuine. Relatives or the accomplice could have paid the man to produce them.

Johann Carl Franz was found not guilty. Prosecuting counsel, Serjeant Ballantine, later confided in his memoirs that he thought the evidence against Franz, though circumstantial, 'conclusive'. The fact that he was found not guilty Ballantine put down largely to the inexperience of the judge! In his summing up Mr Justice Blackburn had given the impression that 'he was labouring under a sense of hesitation and doubt; and juries, always loth to inflict the penalty of death, were affected by his demeanour'. If that were really the case, it seems incredibly hard on the detectives, particularly Whicher, who yet again, despite all their hard work, fell at a hurdle over which they had no control.

The de Vidil trial came up later that month at the same assizes and before the same judge who, by then, seems to have got into his stride, although as we have seen, again de Vidil was found not guilty of the capital charges. By all accounts Whicher was now an ailing man; but it was Inspector Thornton, Dickens's 'Dornton', who died from a stroke the following month.

14

VINDICATED

JONATHAN WHICHER was to have a curious final adventure when, in 1862, he and Chief Superintendent Walker, the Scotsman whom Charles Dickens had mistaken for a detective, were sent to Warsaw to advise on the setting up of an English-style police force.

At that time Poland, as a country, did not exist. During the eighteenth century, Austria, Prussia, and Russia had carved her up between them — an act not appreciated by the Poles, who wanted their country reunited and never ceased in their efforts to achieve this aim. Warsaw was in the Russian sector, where the continuing unrest led to repression and the withholding of local rule; but in 1855 a liberal new czar, Alexander II, came on the scene, and the iron fist began to unclench. His first act on coming to power had been to liberate the serfs. He then set about achieving reforms in law, politics — and the police. In July 1862 the czar's representative, Colonel Demidoff, called on Sir Richard Mayne requesting advice and assistance. He was given copies of the Receiver's Accounts, the House of Commons Report on Fires in the Metropolis, a Metropolitan Police booklet 'Instructions for Police' — and, as a bonus, the services of Whicher and Walker.

As chief superintendent of the elite A or Whitehall Division, Walker was now an important man. He was a confidant of royals, whom he accompanied on state occasions, and had even spent a week's holiday at Balmoral as reward from a grateful Prince Albert for assistance on a visit to Edinburgh. The emissaries from the Yard must have made a fascinating couple: the wily, rural, down-to-earth detective, Whicher, and the well-educated Presbyterian and temperance man, Walker, son of a lawyer, whose adequate means made practising unnecessary.

Administrative reforms proved insufficient to stem the unrest, and when Walker and Whicher arrived in Warsaw serious trouble was already brewing. There had even been an attempt to assassinate the brother of the czar, the grand duke Constantine, who was in overall command. The men from Scotland Yard wrote home, from their room in the Hotel Europe, that they thought the authorities (with whom they were in daily touch) were well pleased with the information they had imparted — although no change had yet been made in the existing police system.

> Everything seems very quiet, and no further attempts at assassination have been made, altho' it is feared similar acts will be repeated, but every precaution is taken to prevent them. Indeed, the government appears to be in constant apprehension.
>
> Our mission here is kept entirely secret except to the three gentlemen we have been in communication with, that being deemed the most prudent course under existing circumstances, — as our personal safety might be endangered by a wrong construction being placed on the object of our visit.
>
> R. W. WALKER
J. WHICHER

On their return to London, the grand duke's aide wrote Sir Richard a fulsome letter, complimenting him on the justice and sagacity of the remarks of his two policemen and the practical utility of their information and instruction. Their visit had been entirely satisfactory, and fresh proof of the degree of perfection which all branches of public service had attained in England. How much use was ever made of all that imparted wisdom is not known, although a senior officer later commented that Walker and Whicher had found the customs so very different that they believed the English police system could not be successfully introduced there. The following year the expected uprising took place and was brutally repressed.

Inspector Whicher retired on pension in March 1864, suffering from 'congestion of the brain' — the last of Scotland Yard's pioneer detectives. On Thornton's death in 1861, Frederick Williamson had been promoted in his stead, and the following two or three years saw a flurry of new appointments, mostly of educated, bilingual men, some of whom went straight into the Branch on joining the force. Twenty-seven-year-old James Jacob Thomson had studied the new science of electricity, been assistant secretary to an Indian prince, joined the Met in 1856, left for the Devon constabulary six months later, then transferred to the Hampshire force, and now wanted to come back to London — scarcely a steady work record, but he did also speak French, Italian, and Greek, having been born in the Middle East of a Scottish merchant father and an Italian mother famous for her international *soirées*. Then there was the suave and smartly dressed 22-

year-old, Nathaniel Druscovitch, who was of Polish extraction and also fluent in several languages. Perhaps one of the Yard's oddest appointees was Edwin Coathupe, a 26-year-old surgeon who had been educated in Germany and studied medicine in Bristol before taking a fancy to detective work. Coathupe stayed only three years, went back to doctoring, then became head of detectives and deputy chief constable of Manchester city, and later chief constable of Bristol City Police.

Considering that the qualifications for joining the Metropolitan Police at that time were merely that candidates had to be under 30 years of age, standing 5ft. 7in. *clear* without shoes or stockings, of strong constitution, free of any bodily complaint, generally intelligent and able to read and write, the attractions of the branch were clearly pulling in some above-average applicants who were a far cry from ex-labourers and butchers such as Whicher and Smith. However, one or two of their ilk still made it, such as the uneducated West Countryman, John Shore. At twenty-four, Shore had two years service in Bristol City behind him when he joined the Metropolitan Police, where he became a detective sergeant within two years, earning the 'John Blunt' designation 'for his bluff and breezy manner'.[1] Shore became the terror of the race-course thieves and pickpockets, which is perhaps a clue as to why he was appointed, as at that time London was in the terrifying grip of footpads and garrotters.

By now, the department was under the control of two men in their mid-30s: Frederick Williamson and the keen and lively Richard Tanner, who, according to a contemporary, Timothy Cavanagh, was a great favourite of Sir Richard Mayne. 'Dick' Tanner had come into the Branch in 1854 as a P C clerk, having seen service as a constable amongst the glitter and vice of the C or St James's Division which covered the West End of London. Tanner liked to 'keep a book' on the allocation of cases and his colleagues' chances of promotion, but his energies were soon put to better use when he was appointed sergeant in the department. He soon, says Cavanagh, 'became not only a strong favourite, but one of its best officers'. A good hand was essential to a clerk in those days, when official reports were all handwritten by them—often from almost illegible scribbles submitted—so it is very likely that the elegantly written notebook in the Metropolitan Police Museum, *Prisoners apprehended by Richard Tanner from July 1856 to 1867*, is in his own writing. The first-person contents give an interesting insight into the continuing work of the Branch over those

[1] *The Police Review and Parade Gossip*, 18 March 1898.

years — particularly as Tanner appends 'Remarks' to the précis of each of his cases.

When available, the detectives continued to do duty at Epsom race-course and London's theatres, from the Alhambra Palace to Her Majesty's Opera House. They also attended any event at which crowds gathered, from thanksgiving services in Westminster Abbey to the parade which followed the Queen's awarding of the Victoria Cross to Crimean War heroes in Hyde Park. The Yard men did not have it all their own way when working among crowds. One Derby Day, Tanner was soundly kicked by a man he was arresting for possession of three handkerchiefs, knowing them to be stolen. On another, while he was attempting to take a man for posses-sion of a stolen overcoat, a gang of thieves rescued his quarry. Tanner arrested Flash Jimmy — the booth-owner who had incited them — instead.

Preventing prize fights could be an even more dangerous duty. Sergeant Smith and Tanner tried to halt 'a fight got up between two toughs', but Sergeant Smith got into an argument with one of the jockeys in the crowd. The little man complained to Travers, a pugilist who in this instance was acting as second; 'he came up', wrote Dick Tanner in his notebook, 'and struck me on the nose and felled me to the ground insensible.'

Other regular customers were deserters and passers of counterfeit coin. The penalty for the latter offence was severe. A barman caught by Tanner selling false coinage went down for ten years' penal servitude. More counterfeit money had been found at the man's home, and his wife was also arrested but later set free due to Tanner's intervention: 'She explained to me that her husband had repeatedly ill-used her for not selling the bad money, I represented this to the magistrate and she was discharged in consequence.'

Nearby government offices occasionally called upon the services of the detectives. Tanner arrested Edward Wellington Boate for embezzling about £40 from the Foreign Office, and he and Thornton took Wellington Guernsey into custody for stealing an ambassadorial dispatch from the library of the Colonial Office. Guernsey, who had served as a provost marshal during the Crimean War, had been refused an appointment by the Colonial Secretary, Sir Edward Lytton Bulwer.[2] The old soldier had access to the library 'from where he stole the dispatch no doubt to annoy Sir

---

[2] The author and playwright who, under the name of Bulwer Lytton, wrote historical and 'Newgate' novels featuring crime and criminals. He was another close friend of Charles Dickens, who named his seventh son Edward Bulwer Lytton Dickens.

DO YOU WISH TO AVOID BEING STRANGLED!!

If so, try our Patent Antigarotte Collar, which enables Gentlemen to walk the streets of London in perfect safety at all hours of the day or night.

EFFECT OF THE ANTIGAROTTE COLLAR ON A GARROTTEER

An epidemic of garrotting during the 1860s brought forth anti-garrotting collars. Note the policeman disappearing into the cellar — doubtless for a cup of tea with the cook or below-stairs maid. (Courtesy of *Punch*)

Franz Muller, the first railway murderer. Arrested by Inspector Tanner after a transatlantic dash, he was executed in 1864.

Edward Lytton and sent it to the *Daily News* newspaper by whom it was published'.

Art world squabbles entered the detectives' sphere surprisingly often. Tanner himself took into custody a painter who wilfully damaged a picture belonging to the Baroness Burdett Coutts; Raphael Monte, 'an artist and sculptor of great fame' (which has not survived to this day) for fraudulent conversion of a marble bust; and an Italian artist who tried a spot of blackmail on his young lady sitter, who had fallen in love with him and written some indiscreet letters. The latter got three years' penal servitude, while a man who blackmailed a gentleman named William D'Arcy, by threatening to accuse him of buggering a young boy, was given a life sentence. When a young soldier was accused of stealing a gold watch from a Count Waldheim, Tanner informed the magistrates that he thought the aristocrat had taken the young man to his lodgings for an improper purpose, and the prisoner was 'discharged in consequence'.

Tanner's next case, a year after his promotion to inspector, was to make his reputation. It began at Hackney one July evening in 1864, when two young bank clerks entered a first-class carriage of the Highbury-bound North London Railway and found its cushions wet and sticky. After touching them they were horrified to see that their hands were red. It was blood. There proved to be blood, too, on the door and its handle, on a silver-topped cane found under the seat, and on a hat on the floor. The guard acted promptly, locking the carriage door, asking the gentlemen for their names and addresses, and telegraphing headquarters.

Twenty minutes later, the driver of a train heading in the opposite direction saw a 'dark mound' on the track ahead and managed to stop his train within a few feet of the obstruction. The mound proved to be the body of a man; alive, but unconscious, and terribly battered about the head. P C Duggan of K Division was soon on the scene and searched the man's pockets, to find four sovereigns, ten shillings and sixpence in silver, some keys, a silver snuff-box, and some correspondence addressed to Thomas Briggs, Clapton Square, Hackney.

Mr Briggs's son soon arrived and identified the injured man as his 70-year-old father, and the chief clerk at the same bank in which the two young men who had raised the alarm were employed. Later, Mr Briggs junior also identified the walking stick and a small travelling bag found in the apartment. But the hat was a puzzle. It was stubby and oddly shaped. His father always wore a tall silk topper made for him by Dignance, a high-class hatters in the City. This was missing, as was Mr Briggs's gold watch and chain. The following day the elderly bank clerk died without regaining consciousness, and Britain had its first railway murder.

Inspector Richard Tanner lost no time in having drawings of the unusual hat posted outside police and railway stations, together with the offer of a £100 reward for information. The bank and the railway soon added another £100. He also circulated pawnbrokers and jewellers with details of the missing watch and chain, and sent his men out visiting hatters. Three days after the finding of the body, a jeweller by the name of Death reported that on the previous day a young man with a foreign accent, probably German, had brought him a gold watch-chain to be valued. He had seemed disappointed with his quote of £3 10s. but, oddly, instead of wanting to sell it, the young man asked for it to be exchanged for another chain. Briggs junior identified the chain left by the young man as that belonging to his father. Unfortunately, the jeweller could not offer much of a description, as the young foreigner had stayed in the shadows within the shop.

It was to be over a week before Tanner was to get his real break, when a cab-driver by the name of Matthews came forward. He claimed he had only just seen a poster about the crime, and recognized the name 'Death' as that on a jeweller's box with which his daughter had been playing. It had been given to her by an acquaintance of theirs, Franz Müller, a young German tailor. Not only that, the description of the hat fitted the one worn by his friend. He knew for certain because he had acquired it for him from Walker's, a firm on his cab route. Moreover, the cabby had the address of Müller's lodgings in Hackney — and a photograph of him. But the bird had flown — to the United States. The resident family were certain of this because they had received a letter from their mild-mannered, kind, and affectionate ex-lodger, posted on board the sailing ship *Victoria*, just before its departure four days earlier. All he had left behind was an empty Walker's hat box; but it was not a sudden flight: their lodger had been talking about his intention to emigrate for at least two weeks. True, it had been on the day after the attack on Mr Briggs that, full of good spirits, he had told them he had at last sufficient money to make the journey.

The electric telegraph could not reach out to sea, so there was no way of verifying that Müller was, indeed, on board the *Victoria*, but rapid pursuit seemed advisable, none the less. Fortunately for Tanner and unfortunately for Müller there was a much quicker way of crossing to the United States — by steamship. With him, on board the fast *SS City of Manchester*, Tanner took the 45-year-old detective, Sergeant George Clarke, the jeweller, Mr Death, and the cabman, Matthews, together with an extradition warrant signed by Mr Henry, the chief magistrate, who had been closely involved with the framing of the extradition laws. They reached New York nearly three weeks ahead of the *Victoria*.

Tanner talked freely to the American Press, with the result that the case was causing as much sensation there as here, and the gaff was nearly blown when sightseers began calling up to the newly arrived *SS Victoria* asking to see 'Müller the murderer'. In Müller's belongings were found a silk hat and a heavy gold watch of the type which had belonged to Thomas Briggs.

Britain was unpopular in the USA at the time, due to allegations that she had been actively supporting the rebellious South by building ships to run the blockade and sink Northern merchantmen. This antagonism was much played upon by a defence attorney provided by the German American Society. Why should they honour an extradition treaty with a country with which they were almost at war? But Commissioner Newton, in whose hands the decision lay, opted for honouring the treaty, and found there was enough evidence to extradite. Five days later the British party left with Müller for England, and Bow Street court, where all such cases initially were heard.

If, as *The Times* had reported, 'the greatest excitement had prevailed' on the arrest in New York, it was nothing to what awaited the seemingly detached Müller in Liverpool and London. Crowds waited daily around Euston Station, hoping for a glimpse of him, even though they had heard how disappointed the American crowds had been by his appearance, which they had expected to be fierce but found, in fact, rather pathetic. After the 'general expectation' of his arrival at Euston had been disappointed on the Friday night, *The Times* warned its readers that, to avoid 'commotion', arrangements had been made for the party to leave the train at Camden station or by a private outlet in Seymour Street. Huge crowds then assembled at Camden as well as Euston, 'opinion being divided as to which of the two he would alight at'. In the event, the party went through to Euston, but were joined by Williamson and Sergeant Thomas when the train halted at Camden.

The moment Müller stepped on the platform at Euston, in 'a light, jaunty manner', he was 'assailed with groans' (boos were not yet fashionable) and 'amid a scene of tumult' and many 'manifestations of popular indignation' he was driven off to Bow Street, which was also under siege.

When it came to the committal and trial the hatters, Dignance, were called to prove that, although shorter, the hat which Müller had carried off to a new life in America was indeed the one they had made for Mr Briggs.

169

Müller had left his own at the scene of the crime, and had picked up Mr Briggs's taller silk topper. This had been cut down — not by a hatter, but by someone who sewed neatly. And Müller was a tailor. 'Müller Cut-Downs' became fashionable for a while. John Death, the jeweller, had positively identified Müller, as had the cab-driver, Matthews. There was soon some suspicion that the latter could have been party to the deed; but it was Müller alone who was found guilty and hanged.

The Metropolitan Police also had their headgear changed in 1864 — from the tall topper to a helmet not so different from today's version. Their swallow-tailed coats went too, to be replaced by tunics of a more military style. The carrying of umbrellas had been forbidden a few years earlier. The low-key look was going. The following year, the American Civil War came to an end. President Lincoln was assassinated, Tolstoy's *War and Peace* was published, ex-Inspector Field had his pension restored, and ex-Inspector Whicher's detective instincts were vindicated.

Field, whom the Press had continued to refer to as an inspector and a member of the Detective Police long after his departure from that body, had, in 1861, finally gone too far — or, rather, was seen to have gone too far. The Home Office had been informed that he had been writing to the Rotterdam Police purporting to be a superintendent in the foreign department of the *Bureau de Sûreté*. His pension was withdrawn as 'no connexion of any kind can be permitted to exist between the Metropolitan Police and a person carrying on unauthorized practices'. It was restored six months later, on promises that he give no further cause for disapprobation or any pretence that he had connection with the government. But the old actor could not help himself — after all, hadn't he been able to pretend to be whoever he liked when he was a police officer? He was soon in trouble again; but finally, in September 1865, he cut his connection with the private enquiry office, and, promising to remain so disconnected, he was allowed to retain his pension.

The dangers of acquiring the habit of deceit so as to become a better detective had not been missed by Charles Dickens. As a later commentator pointed out:[3]

> Bucket poses problems which clearly teased Dickens. What are the ethics proper to a detective? When (if ever) can lying and treachery serve higher truth? How far need a man's profession commit him to guile? Bucket is a man of natural friendliness and good nature who

[3] A. E. Dyson, Macmillan, *Dickens' Bleak House*, 1969.

uses these qualities most unscrupulously in his work. To all appearances they become, therefore, their diabolical opposites, a proof that warmth and good nature can never be 'known'. Bucket is like Tulkinghorn[4] in that he enjoys his power over the people he probes, and is not above playing cat and mouse.

ON 25 APRIL 1865, Inspector Frederick Williamson was called to Bow Street police court where, assembled in a private room, were the chief magistrate, a clergyman, an elderly woman from a religious order, and a heavily veiled young woman—Constance Kent come to confess to the murder of her step-brother Francis. Since the crime five years earlier, Constance had been living in a French convent and, later, at a religious retreat in Brighton, where she had had the time to contemplate her deeds. It must have been a poignant moment for Williamson, who is said to have had great regard for Whicher, and who had been deeply upset by the sad end to his mentor's career. At the trial, Whicher is reported to have been a dignified though infirm figure.

Like Inspector Field, Whicher was soon to be immortalized in print. In 1868 was published what T. S. Eliot referred to as 'the first, the longest and the best of the modern English detective novels'—*The Moonstone* by Dickens's close friend and collaborator, Wilkie Collins. In his book, *Bloody Murder*, Julian Symons disputes the 'first' claim, which he thinks belongs to *The Notting Hill Mystery* (1862) by Charles Felix. He also feels that the skills of Whicher, like those of Field, were much exaggerated, but that 'Collins may have had in mind his rehabilitation'.

The two fictional detectives have much in common. Sergeant Cuff's walk is 'soft' as Bucket's must surely be, given the manner in which he tends to materialize on the scene without anyone noticing his approach. Both men are confident, decisive, self-possessed, and skilled in extracting information from people without them being aware it is happening. Both have all-seeing eyes. Sergeant Cuff's steely, light grey variety had, Collins tells his readers, 'a very disconcerting trick, when they encountered your eyes, of looking as if they expected something more from you than you were aware of yourself'. However, Cuff is not an ebullient figure like Bucket—quite the reverse. His voice is melancholy, his skin withered as an autumn leaf, his style dry and low-key, and he is given to oblique utterings. 'He might have been a parson or an undertaker—or anything else you like, except what he really was.'

4 A solicitor.

Collins's previous mystery novel, *The Woman in White*, had proved immensely popular. Consequently, *The Moonstone* received a great deal of public attention; but Dickens and he were not first in the field internationally. The French police chief Eugène Vidocq, whose memoirs were published in 1828, and Edgar Allan Poe, the American writer of chilling tales which began to appear in 1839, are considered to be the grandfather and father of the detective story, and French writer Émile Gaboriau the father of the detective novel with his *L'Affaire Lerouge* (1866). Great public interest in real-life police detectives had also led to the publication of several books purporting to be the real-life memoirs of English detectives. These included the popular *Recollections of a Detective Police Officer* by 'Waters' (1856), *Experiences of a Real Detective* by Inspector 'F' (1862), and *The Autobiography of an English Detective* (1863)—all written by a man named William Russell. The year (1860) of Whicher's failure at Road had seen the publication of *The Detective's Notebook* and *The Diary of an Ex-Detective*, both books purporting to be by Charles Martell but in fact being the work of a man named Thomas Delf.

The Woman in White had no police detective; but in *The Moonstone* Sergeant Cuff not only emerges, much trumpeted, on the scene a quarter of the way through, but dominates the narrative for another 100 pages. Although Dickens never actually admitted that Field was Bucket (although a friend, who felt Dickens exaggerated the detective's abilities, admitted that there was something of Bucket in Field), there is no doubt that Whicher and his experiences at Road deeply influenced the writing of *The Moonstone*.

The plot of the novel revolves, not around a murder, but around the theft of a diamond and the consequences of that act. Cuff, all persistence and stealthy deduction, and for whom no clue is too small to follow, is called in when the bumbling provincial policeman Superintendent Seegrave fails to make adequate headway. The fictional version does, however, make his contempt for the local man clear, while Whicher swore to the commissioner that he had been the soul of diplomacy. The setting for the crime in Collins's mystery is a large country house teeming with family, servants, and guests, all of whom act as suspects. Pivotal to the plot is a teenage girl (the daughter of the house, whom Cuff early suspects as being the culprit), and a futile search for a nightdress stained with paint rather than blood takes up a great deal of time. Physically, Cuff is unlike Whicher, and the author makes an effort to imbue his policeman with a definite character by giving him a fanatical interest—in rose-growing (actually Williamson, whom Collins probably met, enjoyed growing roses) — and little personal idiosyncrasies such as a tendency to whistle *The Last Rose of Summer* while deep in his deductions.

Again, as with Whicher in the Constance Kent case, Cuff's involvement ends inconclusively — in this case half-way through the book — Cuff being quite satisfied in his mind that the girl is the guilty party, while she and her family successfully obstruct him in proving this. The mystery is solved after Cuff reappears towards the end of the novel. By now he is happily retired, and has metamorphosed from a character with the air of an undertaker into a countryman, complete with shooting jacket, broad-brimmed white hat, and stout walking stick. It has become obvious that the girl is not guilty after all, and Cuff happily admits to his previous error, saying that it is only in books that the officers of the detective force 'are superior to the weakness of making a mistake'. This is a bit rich given the utter certainty with which he had made his previous pronouncements, but he blithely goes on to make another — which, this time, proves correct.

What the now retired and vindicated Inspector Whicher thought of all this is not on record, but one presumes it must have afforded him some comfort. The impression is sometimes given that he died soon after the confession of Constance Kent, but in fact he lived on for a further 16 years, and carried out some of the complex private enquiry work on the case of the Tichborne Claimant after his retirement. Jonathan Whicher, 'a man who in his day, achieved considerable eminence',[5] died at Wandsworth in 1881 at the age of 66.

Four years later, a 'small, mouse-like little creature . . . this insignificant, inoffensive little person'[6] — Constance Kent — was released from prison, where she had been sent after her death sentence had been commuted 20 years before.

---

[5] *Police Guardian.*
[6] As described by her prison governor — who was also the writer, Major Arthur Griffiths.

15

OUTRAGE!

THE THREE MILITARY BANDSMEN were in the habit of meeting for supper or a drink after their performances in the orchestras of West End theatres, and the evening of Friday, 27 September 1867 was no exception. They were causing no disturbance, so were surprised when later, as they meandered homewards along the southern side of Bloomsbury Square, a couple of men lounging on the corner made honking noises at them and called them ' — pigs'. Henry Furber, one of the bandsmen, was just turning round to look at them when he felt a push, and his hat was knocked off. Stooping to retrieve it, he was even more startled to hear a bang, see a flash, and catch out of the corner of his eye the sight of his fellow Life Guard,[1] Eddie M'Donnell, toppling to the ground exclaiming, 'I've been shot!'

Furber gave chase but lost the two attackers, then returned to help his friend. Afterwards, he could remember only that the man who fired the shot was tall, with a long fair beard and short hair. The seriously wounded M'Donnell was taken to University College Hospital where, soon afterwards, Mr Flowers, the Bow Street magistrate, attended to witness his statement.

The cry 'another Fenian Outrage!' went out over the land; but curiously enough, it was soon being suggested that M'Donnell had not been shot because he was a British soldier but probably because he resembled a Fenian informer, thought to be in the area under the guard of two detectives. This trio were supposed to have just left a pub around the same time as the bandsmen. 'These Irishmen,' speculated *The Times* the following Monday, 'probably imagining by their upright walk that the bandsmen were detective policemen in plain clothes, attacked them.'

At that time Britain was in a state of considerable unrest, due partly to

---

[1] The Life Guards are one of the two regiments which form the Household Calvary. The first and second troops of Life Guards horse were amalgamated in 1922.

high unemployment and rising prices, but also to the flowering of Irish republicanism both in Ireland and among the Irish living on the mainland. The Irish Republican Brotherhood, founded in Dublin in 1858, was given financial support by the American Fenian Brotherhood, many of whom were still full of hatred for the English as a result of their enforced emigration following the famine of the 1840s. When the American Civil War came to an end, the Fenians were also able to supply arms, ammunition, and military expertise.

An uprising led by the IRB leader Colonel Kelly, late of the Unionist Army, was planned to take place in Ireland early in 1867. Diversions and the acquisition of additional arms were to be organized in England by Captain Richard O'Sullivan Burke. A much-travelled man, Burke had seen service not only with the Unionists in the American Civil War but earlier with the South Cork militia and, oddly, the Chilean cavalry. The 1867 rebellion collapsed, as had an arms raid on the poorly guarded arsenal at Chester Castle. The latter failure was due to several factors: the attention drawn by the startlingly sudden influx of hundreds of Irishmen into that sedate city; the fact that the man who was to lead them failed to arrive in time because his train was late; and the fact that at the last minute an informer named John Corydon gave the game away.

On 11 September 1867, Colonel Kelly and his aide were arrested in Manchester as they were attempting to clear up a casual internal squabble. At first the police were unaware of who they had in their hands, and merely charged the men with a minor offence under the Vagrancy Act. But enquiries in Ireland and positive identification by John Corydon soon changed that situation. The Manchester police, however, were not to retain their major prize for long. The prison van in which Kelly and his colleague were being transported to gaol was ambushed, and Police Sergeant Brett (who refused to relinquish his keys) was shot dead. The Fenian leaders were rescued, but five of the ambush gang were caught. They were awaiting trial when bandsman M'Donnell was shot as he strolled towards his home that autumn evening.

James Jacob Thomson, the detective of many tongues and now promoted to inspector, arrested a clerk named John Groves, who admitted being in the area at the time. Groves had Fenian papers among his belongings and a pistol, into the chambers of which fitted the bullet which had struck M'Donnell. In addition, an informer identified Groves as the man who had been following and threatening to shoot him. The suspect was taken to M'Donnell's bedside at University College Hospital, but although his features seemed right to the injured man, M'Donnell thought his attacker had been taller — despite the fact, Inspector Thomson pointed out to the bandsman, somewhat ghoulishly, that this might be because be was now lying down. Groves was remanded in custody for a week and, it seems, the police were determined that a Manchester-style rescue was not to be repeated. According to the *Illustrated Police News*, which may have been exaggerating, about 60 Irish Americans had posted themselves near the entrance to Bow Street.

> These men are said to be easily recognisable by the peculiarity of their walk and their attire. . . . Police authorities made very elaborate preparations for the safe conduct of the prisoners for the van was escorted by quite a cavalcade of armed officers as it proceeded on its way to the House of Detention in Clerkenwell. Before and beside the van rode some dozen mounted policemen armed with swords and revolvers while within it were seated Superintendent Durkin, Inspector Thomson of the Detective Force, and three other constables also carrying revolvers and, on the top, five other constables kept guard. Immediately following were three cabs loaded within and without with policemen — a display of strength which was well calculated to deter any attempt at rescue by the way.

M'Donnell had been shot in the chest, the bullet passing straight through him. Although his condition was not at first too severe and indeed improved, 'with the change in the weather, however', *The Times* had to report five days later, 'depressing symptoms appeared'. These were of pleurisy and were to be followed by pneumonia, which resulted in poor M'Donnell passing away a couple of days later and the charge turning into one of murder. It was easier to kill someone in the days before penicillin.

The case against Groves, never a strong one, fell apart after a sensational new witness under cross-examination showed obvious signs of being deranged, and it was shown that the bullet, whilst it might be squeezed into the chamber of the pistol, would not, in fact, go through the barrel. The charge was withdrawn, and it appears that there was no further action. (According to R. V. Comerford,[2] Kelly, 'a natural gunman', did in fact set up an assassination squad which made attempts on the lives of informers and detectives during this period.) Police still had access to several informers in the Fenian camp, however, and Thomson was soon to make an arrest which would ensure him lasting fame within the department.

---

[2] *The Fenians in Context.*

Intelligence had been emerging that serious arms-buying had been going on in Birmingham, supposedly on behalf of the Chilean government. The buyers, however, bore a curious resemblance to the Fenian leader, Captain Burke, and his aide, Casey. At the very time when desperate, last-minute attempts were being made to gain clemency for the men sentenced to be hanged for the Manchester ambush, an informer named Devany told Thomson that Britain's second most wanted man was staying in the same lodgings as him, in Tavistock Street near Tottenham Court Road.

While Burke and Casey were out walking, Devany identified them. Thomson called upon the assistance of a passing P C and arrested the pair. There was a scuffle in which Burke broke away, whereupon Thomson drew a revolver and shouted, 'By God, Burke, if you don't stop I will fire on you!' Burke, said to be a light-hearted and humorous fellow, stopped in his tracks and said, 'Don't do anything desperate.' Eventually, they managed to hail cabs to take them to Bow Street. The two men were charged with treason felony and sent, on remand, to Clerkenwell House of Detention.

There must have been less provocative places in which to lodge the prisoners. Clerkenwell (and nearby Holborn), besides having a substantial Irish population, was historically a Radical area and still a centre for Chartism and the Reform League, many of whose members sympathized with the plight of the Irish. Meetings had been held on Clerkenwell Green and petitions drawn up in support of the men who, a couple of days after the arrest of Burke, were to become 'the Manchester Martyrs' when the pleas for clemency failed for three of them and they were hanged. As expected, there was plenty of information warning of possible attempts to rescue Burke and Casey. The police response was to put two or three policemen on guard around the perimeter wall.

At about ten minutes to four on the afternoon of Friday, 13 December 1867, Inspector Thomson was leaving the Clerkenwell House of Detention in a hansom cab, after taking in a witness from Birmingham to identify the prisoners. As he did so, one of three persons loitering outside rushed up to the vehicle to have a better look at Thomson's companion. The cab had not gone very far when a deafening explosion rent the air — so loud, in fact, that it was heard 40 miles away. This was not surprising considering the amount of gunpowder used — said to be 548lb. packed into a 36-gallon beer cask.

While exercising in the prison yard each afternoon between three and four o'clock, Captain Burke had spotted a weakness in the wall. He devised a plan whereby, after warning him by throwing a white ball over the wall, his sympathisers would blow a huge hole in it through which he could escape. All had been made ready on 12 December. The barrow holding the beer cask was leaning against the prison wall and the white ball was thrown — but the fuse would not light. The whole enterprise was starting to draw attention and was temporarily abandoned. On the following day it did succeed, but by then Mayne had received more specific information about the time and place of the attempt — although not the date. The previous evening he had sent Thomson to warn the governor, who changed the exercise arrangements, thus causing the Fenians to fail in their rescue attempt. What they did manage to do was to demolish tenements opposite, causing, ultimately, the death of six people, two of whom were children, and the maiming of many more.

It transpired that some of the policemen had carefully observed the activity around the walls (one, in fact, had warned the governor about it and another was approaching the bomb when it exploded, throwing him backwards, insensible, and rendering him permanently deaf). They had even seen the beer cask without realizing its significance. Afterwards, they were at least stung into sufficient activity to arrest three running people, although one of these (who was beaten by his captor) turned out to be a police spy and informer. The remaining two were charged but found not guilty. In fact, the only man to be convicted and hanged for the offence was Michael Barrett. He had been arrested later in Glasgow and, while probably telling the truth in claiming he did not place the bomb or light the fuse, was obviously involved in the plot.

At the inquest on 'the Clerkenwell Outrage', Inspector Thomson proved remarkably frank about the dusty response he had received from Captain Codd, the prison governor, when advising him of the specific rescue threat, and of Mayne's suggestion that the two prisoners be exercised separately. 'The Governor told me to return his thanks to Sir Richard Mayne, but as regards the internal arrangements of the prison he was quite competent to provide for them, and did not want any suggestions.' Later, Thomson claimed, Captain Codd called him into his office and in the presence of his chief warder told him to tell Sir Richard to mind his own business, saying that he did not believe that the prison would be attacked. He hoped he might live until it was, and he would be pretty sure to live to a ripe old age. 'I told Sir Richard Mayne what the Governor had said . . . but made no mention of the offensive expressions.' The coroner remarked that he just wished they had got together and done something about protecting

(*Above*) Two of the detectives sent to prison as a result of the Turf Frand scandal: Inspector Meiklejohn (*left*) and Chief Inspector Druscovitch.

(*Right*) Sir Richard Mayne, KCB, towards the end of his 39 years' service as commissioner. Joint Commissioner Rowan retired in 1850, and was replaced by Captain William Hay, who proved unable to co-operate with Mayne. Following Hay's death in 1855, Mayne was to hold the post alone until he died in 1868.

the prison. He particularly criticized Mayne, as did everyone else, for not sending more men to protect the exterior.

The incident helped complete a miserable final chapter in Mayne's long and dedicated career. Only the previous year, the now ill and elderly commissioner had borne heavy criticism for putting into effect the Home Secretary's order banning a demonstration by the Reform League in Hyde Park. A riot had ensued, during which the police suffered heavy and, in some cases, serious casualties. Mayne was currently being sued for libel by an ex-public carriage office inspector — one of three he had sacked for mishandling of expense accounts — and a much-loved daughter had died.

After Clerkenwell the Press, constantly critical of him, had a field day, admittedly with some justification. He was too old for the job and increasingly autocratic. Ex-Chief Inspector Timothy Cavanagh, in his book *Scotland Yard Past and Present*, describes how he was kept standing to attention before Mayne, who continued writing for ten minutes before deigning to look up, fix Cavanagh with his hawk-like eye, and coldly confirm his promotion, adding that he hoped the young man would give satisfaction. 'Respected but feared by all in the service' is how Cavanagh remembered the thin-faced man with 'a very hard, compressed mouth'. After the Clerkenwell débâcle Mayne offered his resignation. It was not accepted but it made little difference. Shortly afterwards he died.

Another consequence of the outrage was that the Metropolitan Police were swamped with mail reporting further Fenian plots, all of which had to be taken seriously and followed through. At least, every police station was connected to the electric telegraph, and the headings on many official forms were actually printed, making it no longer necessary for clerks to draw elaborate divisional letters on them. In any event, the force itself was too small and the Detective Branch, with its 15 members, ludicrously so, particularly now that it had the extra burden of monitoring Fenian activities.

The cessation of transportation to the colonies[3] meant that more desperate and hardened criminals were being released back onto the streets of London after completion of their sentences. Their numbers had been a contributory factor to the serious outbreak of garrotting in 1862. Its incidence had been reduced since that time by ferocious sentences and liberal use of the lash, but sporadic outbursts continued. Indeed, at the same time as the Clerkenwell Outrage inquest was being reported, a 'Fatal Garotte

[3] Transportation to New South Wales ended in 1840, to Tasmania in 1853, and to Western Australia in 1868.

Outrage' was also in the news, although it does appear that the actual death of the victim — the chief oil cooper at St Katherines Dock — was caused by asphyxiation and heart failure due to his chest being kneeled upon by his attackers.

Following the police failure at Clerkenwell, Mayne had requested an increase in manpower and, particularly, for more detectives. The Home Office set up a departmental committee on the organization of the Metropolitan Police; and to illustrate how long, complex, and unpredictable a case could become, Inspector Thomson submitted an outline of the development of one of his own: the tracking down of the Great Stamp Robbers.

In May 1866, thieves had broken into the Inland Revenue office in Manchester and made off with £10,000 worth of stamps. When Thomson arrived on the scene it had already been searched by the local police, who informed him there was nothing more to be found. But this did not satisfy the man from the Yard: 'I knew from experience that when thieves are engaged on an important burglary, they often suffer from looseness of the bowels. So I looked about for any deposits there might be and I found three.' Under some bricks, he found *Wright's Racing Calendar* for that very month, May, and he also noticed that two eggs had been broken on the step of the outside entrance.

Despite every effort by the London detectives, however, there was no movement in the case until a man named Batt tried to claim money for one of the stamps and was arrested and charged. Thomson instructed two of his men to keep watch at Bow Street to see whether anyone tried to communicate with Batt. Sure enough, as he was being shepherded into the prison van, a one-legged man shoved a twist of tobacco into Batt's hand. He was Richard Shaw, or Peg-Leg Dick, and Thomson promptly leaned on him to turn 'approver'. It was a move which, although ultimately successful, must have caused Thomson some moments of doubt. 'A more trying man I had never come across', he confides in his report. 'He was untruthful, he was seldom sober; he was always filthy and he persecuted me day and night by coming to my house and if I was not at home, he would lie on the doorstep, dead drunk.'

However, Peg-Leg Dick did help Thomson track down 'Bill', one of the stamp-thieves, at Lewes races. Thomson glanced at the man whom his informer indicated — and caught his eye.

> and at that moment I felt the force of a lesson which had been taught me when I first had anything to do with the detective police and it was

The multilingual James J. Thomson, one of the second generation of detectives, who was to rise to the rank of superintendent. (Courtesy of Police Review)

The popular Superintendent Frederick Williamson, who was to survive the Turf Fraud Scandal and become the Detective Branch's first chief superintendent.

this, that in following a thief or suspect, you must never let him catch
your eye, because the eye indicated more or less what is passing in your
mind . . . He immediately saw something was wrong and his eye went
over me like a flash of lightning; he was taking a mental photograph of
me from head to foot; he saw danger in me to him.

Since part of the object was get 'Bill' to lead them to the brains of the
gang, one 'Tom', Thomson withdrew, but soon afterwards was able to
arrest another suspect. The evidence against this man was slender,
however, and to hold him it was necessary to put Peg-Leg Dick into the
witness box, after which the informer took fright, and it was suggested that
he go to stay with his wife's relatives near Edinburgh. 'This was agreed and
I took the family there. It was a terrible journey; Shaw was drunk for the
whole of it and his family teemed with a foul stench.'

Peg-Leg did, however, suggest that if Thomson cared to pop into the
Doncaster Races on his return journey he might run into Tom and Bill.
The inspector telegraphed Sergeant Thomas, asking him to meet him in
Doncaster, where they finally nailed their quarry. However, Doncaster
Police proved unhelpful when it came to arranging the train journey to
Manchester.

> and it was difficult to get off with anything like safety. We handcuffed
> them together and managed to get a compartment to ourselves but
> then found that there was no light in it so I asked one of the porters to
> get a couple of ginger beer bottles and buy some candles and so we had
> a light for our journey.

Later, at the home of another member of the gang, Thomson found a
number of *Wright's Racing Calendars* and noticed that the one for the
month of May was missing. The matter of the eggs was cleared up when
the thieves explained that they had dropped them on the steps deliberately
so as to prevent groups of youngsters, who often sat there talking and
laughing, from doing so while the office was being burgled. The Inspector
never did explain to what use he put his 'deposit' clue, unless it was that
the racing calendar had been used as toilet paper and he was too delicate to
say so.

Thomson concluded his report to the Home Office committee thus:

> The case occupied some six months and while the leading points have
> been given, it must be appreciated that there were numberless minor
> details; all the anxiety, the calculations, failures and disappointments;
> all the watching, loss of meals, out early and in late, the mishaps and

vexations, getting wet, travelling haphazard by day and night, catching cold and so on . . .

After that, what could the committee do but agree that the Detective Branch should be strengthened? They also agreed to enlarge the force and put more detectives out on the divisions.

It is interesting to compare the work of the Home Office senior civil servants at that time, as experienced by lawyer and Fenian expert Robert Anderson, who was later to become an assistant commissioner. He soon noticed (reports his son, A. P. Moore-Anderson[4]) that the way to get on at the Home Office was to do as little as possible. 'The ordinary work was light, and it was left to an industrious minority. The hours were from 11 a.m. to 5 p.m., a nominal 11 a.m. and a punctual 5 p.m.; much of that time was given to luncheon, gossip and the newspapers; and there was plenty left for games and ragging.'

Colonel Henderson, who replaced Mayne as commissioner, was quick to put the Home Office recommendations into effect. He added to the detective department one superintendent (Williamson), two chief inspectors (Thomson and Clarke), and nine sergeants. Thomson, however, was soon promoted out of the Branch to become a divisional superintendent. As for that promising inspector, Richard Tanner, whom Cavanagh thought destined to be the best man the Detective Branch ever possessed, save Whicher, he 'broke down early' and retired in July 1869 due to 'rheumatism'. His £100-a-year pension was augmented by his takings as landlord of the White Swan hotel at Winchester, but he collapsed and died of apoplexy in 1873.

Andrew Lansdowne, who came into the department as a sergeant at this time, later described how the work was handed out in 'dockets'. 'I often had as many as six to eight enquiries on hand at one time, in different parts of London and outside, without skilled assistance, except what could be given by the plain-clothes men.' For many years, Lansdowne claimed, Williamson had a completely free hand in the way the department was run. But it did not go to his head — he was loved for his kindness and wisdom. 'I never knew his counsel to be wrong.' Timothy Cavanagh could look back a little earlier. He had been in charge of the Yard's 1857 innovation — a hostel for its single men at 1 Palace Place, a small, old-fashioned house in the corner of Great Scotland Yard. 'Dolly' Williamson had always been well to the fore in the jolly japes the lads got up to, Cavanagh observed, but

---

[4] *The Life of Sir Robert Anderson.*

he had the happy knack of staying out of the firing line when trouble loomed. He also showed his more serious side by studying French while others went off to the theatres or other places of entertainment, and, in later years, began learning German.

Superintendent Williamson inspired confidence in another young detective, John George Littlechild, who found his chief unfailingly polite where others could be dictatorial. Admittedly, he could give the impression of being somewhat heavy and unimpressionable, but his grasp of case detail was rapid and he was full of dry humour and anecdotes. Recalled in Littlechild's memoirs with particular pleasure were Sunday mornings, when the urgent work was done and Williamson would come among them in their tiny offices close by his own. (There was one for the sergeants, one for the inspectors, and one for the superintendent.)

But, Lansdowne was to record, the events of 1877 were to shake Mr Williamson's faith in his men and make him 'much less confiding' — and with good cause.

As with most tales of corruption, that of the Turf Fraud Scandal of 1877 is not only depressing but too complex and tedious to recount in detail. Suffice it to say that a gang of turf fraudsters, pretending to have the knowledge to back winners — which wary bookies were preventing them from exercising — made it known that they were happy to help others get rich too, if they would assist in laying bets. The punters thus attracted would eventually place large amounts of their own money — and hear no more. Since 1873, Sergeant Meiklejohn of the detective department had been taking bribes from Kurr, a member of the gang, to help him avoid prosecution in other turf frauds. According to Kurr, it was the sergeant who had actually initiated their crooked partnership. Inspector Druscovitch later became involved when trying to pay off a debt for his brother who was threatened with eviction. Meiklejohn suggested that his trusty and respectable friend, Kurr, might be able to assist.

In 1876, after the fraudsters' success in netting £10,000 from a French aristocrat, the Comtesse de Goncourt, Williamson put Druscovitch on to the case. Meiklejohn had actually been given some of the £10,000 (which proved to be more traceable than the gang had imagined), but when a report on his tendering of the notes came into the detective department, it went to the already compromised Druscovitch. Eventually Williamson, puzzled by their lack of progress, took over the case. Druscovitch, with several other officers, was sent to Holland to bring back one of the gang who had been arrested there. Meanwhile Sergeant Littlechild, sworn to secrecy, was sent to arrest Kurr. This task culminated in the sergeant looking down the barrel of Kurr's revolver after giving chase to him and his companions along a dark road in Islington. Fortunately, Kurr responded to Littlechild's shouted advice not to add murder to his deeds, and released his grip on the weapon. After their conviction and sentencing to long terms of imprisonment, the gang began squealing on the detectives they had had in their pay. According to them, there were four of them: Meiklejohn, Druscovitch, Palmer, and Clarke.

The arrest and trial of these senior detectives for conspiring to obstruct the course of justice caused a sensation. Finally, three of them — Meiklejohn, Druscovitch, and Palmer, were found guilty and sentenced to two years' hard labour. The 60-year-old Clarke, against whom (his counsel suggested) the fraudsters had cooked up a case to nail him for his past successes against their ilk, was acquitted, partly due, no doubt, to Williamson speaking up for him. During his evidence, Superintendent Williamson had also pointed out that detectives were obliged to mix with the worst of characters, and had admitted that it had not been necessary for them to report such meetings unless they proved fruitful. This, allied to their great freedom of movement (meetings with the gang had taken place all over the country), the security they enjoyed in being part of that select firm within a firm, and the fact that they were quite poorly paid, made transgression by some inevitable at some point.

There had also been dissatisfaction with the detectives' performance on some recent murder cases, and it was becoming obvious that the style of department set up for the original eight first detectives was no longer suitable. A Home Office committee opted for an entirely new organization, which came into being in 1878. Among other things, the detectives were to be more highly paid and there were to be many more of them, particularly on the divisions. This localization (despite the continued existence and development of Central Squads) has remained one of the most familiar features of the detective branch. Indeed, as I write there has just been an increase in local detective constables, in an effort to improve the service.

Williamson, who, despite being in charge of the erring detective department, managed to emerge whiter than white, was not called upon to resign but promoted to be the new Department's chief superintendent. But the top job went to a man similar to Richard Mayne, an ambitious young lawyer named Howard Vincent. He had studied and reported on the French detective system, and was now appointed director of the new Criminal Investigations Department. The CID was born.

SOURCES

Public Record Office

Metropolitan Police case files:
  MEPO 3: 40–5, 47, 49, 61–3
Police and Home office files of
  correspondence and registers
  containing personal details of
  police officers, general policy, and
  administration:
MEPO 1, 2, 3; HO 45: 61–5

Newspapers and Journals

The Daily News
The Guardian
Household Words
Illustrated London Life
Illustrated London News
Illustrated Times
Islington Gazette
The Job (Metropolitan Police
  newspaper — series of articles by
  Bernard Brown on the history of
  the Metropolitan Police Divisions,
  published 1987–8)
John Bull
Lloyds Weekly Newspaper
The London Spy
The Manchester Times

The Morning Chronicle
The Morning Herald
The News
The Observer
Police Gazette
The Police Guardian
The Police Recorder
Police Review and Parade Gossip
Punch
The Royal Standard (Windsor, Eton,
  and Slough)
The Sunday Times
The Times
The Weekly Dispatch
The Weekly Times
Cuttings from St Martin's Scrapbook,
  Victoria Public Library, London

Metropolitan Police Museum

Police orders
Divisional registers
Notebook: Prisoners apprehended by
  Richard Tanner from 1856 to 1867
Man from the Yard, unpublished MS
  by Alan R. Pike, OBE
The Pike Collection

SELECT BIBLIOGRAPHY

(Place of publication London, unless otherwise stated.)

Annual Register, or a view of History, Politics and Literature, of the year.

Anon, *Burking the Italian Boy: Fairburn edition of the Trial of John Bishop, Thomas Williams, and John May. Tried at the Old Bailey, Friday 2nd December 1831.* 'Taken in Shorthand', 'Price sixpence'. John Fairburn, 1831. A note with the above, in the British Library, signed by the collector and Dickens authority John F. Dexter (1853–1927), states: 'F. W. Pailthorpe[1] gave me this pamphlet stating that it was "reported" by Charles Dickens and that he had this information from an authoritative source. The description of the prisoners (pp. 21, 22) bears evidence of CD's hand.' This was while the 20-year-old Dickens was engaged in legal reporting, largely at the 'Doctor's Commons', near the Old Bailey.

Anon, *The Detectives' Trial. The Great Detective Case: A condensed history of this remarkable investigation, from its commencement to its present stage, with characteristic sketches of the Principal Personages,* Tinsley Bros.

Anon, *The Illustrated and Unabridged Edition of The Times Report of the Trial of William Palmer,* Ward & Lock

Ballantine, Serjeant, *Some Experiences of a Barrister's Life,* Richard Bentley, 1882

Bridges, Yseult, *Two Studies in Crime,* Jarrolds, 1959

Browne, Douglas G., *The Rise of Scotland Yard,* Harrap, 1956

Cavanagh, ex-Chief Inspector, *Scotland Yard, Past and Present: Experiences of Thirty Seven Years,* Chatto & Windus, 1893

Cobb, Belton, *Critical Years at the Yard: The Career of Frederick Williamson of the Detective Department and the CID,* Faber & Faber, 1956

——, *The First Detectives and the Early Career of Richard Mayne, Commissioner of Police,* Faber & Faber, 1957

Collins, Philip, *Dickens and Crime,* Macmillan, 1962

Collins, Wilkie, *The Woman in White,* first published in serial form in

[1] An (unofficial) illustrator of Dickens's works.

Select Bibliography

Dickens's *All the Year Round* magazine; first published in book form by Collins, 1860

——, *The Moonstone*, with an introduction by G. D. H. and Margaret Cole, London, Collins, 1953

Comerford, R. V., *The Fenians in Context: Irish Politics and Society, 1848–1882*, Dublin, Wolfhound Press, 1984

Dickens, Charles, *Bleak House*, The Oxford Illustrated Dickens, Oxford University Press, 1948 (repr. 1987). First published in serial form by Bradbury & Evans, 1852–3; in book form 1853.

——, *Miscellaneous Papers/Edwin Drood*, Hazell Watson, & Viney, 1933. Dickens's essays have been published in several, often overlapping, collections. These particular 'miscellaneous papers' are a compilation of 'the best' of *Reprinted Pieces* (Dickens essays first published anonymously in Dickens's *Household Words* magazine 1850–6; they include 'The Detective Police' and 'Six Detective Anecdotes', selected by the author for a Library edition in 1858) and *Miscellaneous Papers* (Dickens's essays extracted from *Household Words, All the Year Round, Cornhill Magazine, The Examiner*, his letters to *The Daily News*, etc., selected by the Dickens authority, B. W. Matz, for the National Edition of Dickens published in 1908).

——, *Reprinted Pieces and Others*, Everyman series, Dent, 1920 (repr. 1970). Includes the essay 'On Duty with Inspector Field', not in the above, as well as the other two detective pieces. (All three essays may also be found in *The Uncommercial Traveller and Reprinted Pieces*, Oxford Illustrated Dickens, Oxford University Press, 1958, and reprints.)

Goddard, Henry, *Memoirs of a Bow Street Runner*, Museum Press, 1956

Griffiths, Major Arthur, *Mysteries of Police and Crime*, Cassell, 1898

Hawkins, Sir Henry, *The Reminiscences of Sir Henry Hawkins*, Thomas Nelson & Sons, 1904

Kingston, Charles, *The Law Breakers*, London, John Lane/The Bodley Head, 1930

Lansdowne, Andrew, *A Life's Reminiscences of Scotland Yard*, Leadenhall Press, 1893

Littlechild, Andrew, *The Reminiscences of Chief Inspector Littlechild*, 2nd edn., Leadenhall Press, 1894

Lock, Joan, *Blue Murder*, Hale, 1986

——, *Marlborough Street: The Story of a London Court*, Hale, 1980

——, *Tales from Bow Street*, Hale, 1982

Moore-Anderson, A. P., *The Life of Sir Robert Anderson*, London and Edinburgh, Marshall, Morgan, & Scott, 1947

Quinlivan, Patrick, and Rose, Paul, *The Fenians in London, 1865–1872*, John Calder, 1982

St John Packe, Michael, *The Bombs of Orsini*, Secker & Warburg, 1957

Select Bibliography

Stead, Philip John, *Vidocq: A Biography*, Staple Press, 1953

Symons, Julian, *Bloody Murder: From the Detective Story to the Crime Novel, A History*, Faber & Faber, 1972

Taylor, Bernard, *Cruelly Murdered: Constance Kent and the Killing at Road Hill House*, Souvenir Press, 1979

ACKNOWLEDGEMENTS

My sincere thanks for invaluable advice and assistance are due to the staff of the Metropolitan Police Museum, particularly Richard Sharp and Ken Stone; to the helpful keeper's staff of the local history collections in the Finsbury, Islington Central, Bancroft Road (Tower Hamlets), and Victoria Public Libraries, and the Guildhall and the Scotland Yard Libraries; and also, of course, to the Public Record Office and the British Library at the British Museum and Colindale (Newspaper) Library.

I am also grateful to antiquarian bookseller, John C. G. Hammond, who kindly passed on some of his notes, and to fellow non-fiction crime writer Paul Begg, who similarly obliged me with a couple of details on Jonathan Whicher. Thanks are also due to fellow members of the Crime Writers' Association: to that great book-finder, Marian Babson, who dug out for me one or two beauties; to June Thomson, who lent me some of hers (no greater love . . .); to Jonathan Goodman, who kept a look-out for sources for me and came up with some answers from his great store of crime knowledge; to Don Rumbelow, who found the Charley illustration for me at short notice; to Peter Haining, for the illustrations of Inspector Bucket and that accompanying 'On Duty with Inspector Field'; to David Parker, curator of the Dickens' House Museum for some vital last-minute assistance; and to my friends at *Police Review*, David Pead, Brian Hilliard, and Tony Keep, who patiently allowed me to ferret about among the old issues of *Police Review and Parade Gossip* and assisted in obtaining the picture of J. J. Thomson.

INDEX

Index